Letters of Thomas Jefferson

Th Jefferson

Letters of Thomas Jefferson

selected & edited
with an Introduction
by
FRANK IRWIN

THE SANBORNTON BRIDGE PRESS
Tilton, New Hampshire
1975

Frontispiece: Woodcut by Herschel Logan

Manufactured in the United States of America by The
Sant Bani Press, Inc., Tilton, New Hampshire. Binding
by The New Hampshire Bindery, Concord, New Hampshire.

Library of Congress Catalog Card No. 75-12007

ISBN: 0-89142-022-3

Foreword

ALTHOUGH history sometimes appears to repeat itself, it only rarely evolves a whole series of events in almost precise detail. In the 1790's the Federalists were a war party, ostensibly dedicated to national security. By employing means toward that end which were clearly incompatible with the interests of the American people, they only managed to engineer their own political destruction. During these years the Federalist party passed the Alien and Sedition Laws in an attempt to silence their political opponents. The Customs Service was enlisted in a scheme to spy on private citizens and the mail of citizens was opened illegally. These extensive abuses of authority had their abrupt termination in what has been called the second American Revolution in 1800. In this year Jefferson was elected President by a rather narrow margin. The Federalist party, however, never recovered from this campaign in which they relied heavily upon character assassination and deception. Jefferson was reelected by a landslide vote in 1804 and the Republican party remained in power for many years.

This small collection of Thomas Jefferson's letters includes a substantial number referring to political abuses of which we have more immediate knowledge. An attempt has been made to balance this specially selected material with letters of political and historical interest. Many of Jefferson's letters are retrospective and it would have been extremely difficult to arrange these in any significant chronological order. Under separate chapters this has been done whenever possible.

FRANK IRWIN

Contents

Letters of Thomas Jefferson

Introduction

No ERA in history can be studied in greater detail than
the years immediately preceding and following the
American Revolution. This is primarily due to the extensive correspondence of a few dozen men and particularly
to the thousands of letters written by Thomas Jefferson.
Innumerable incidents in Jefferson's personal life, his political plans and their development, his love of books and
his philosophy, were all projected into this vast area of
communication. His political faith was elemental and has
become a part of our living tradition.

Jefferson has been unequivocally damned by more his-
torians and biographers than any other figure in American
history and the reason for this is to be found in his political
ideas. Some of Jefferson's most fundamental principles cannot be refuted and this advantageous fact has goaded his
enemies for two centuries. The Federalists and their political descendants have played the part of King Canute and,
although they have never quite succeeded in commanding
the tides, they have maintained an undying hatred for the
man who first observed their regularity. Jefferson was one
of the greatest scholars of his time. Over a period of years
he made a comparative study of Republican forms of government in 8th century England, in ancient Saxony, in
Rome and the Greek republics, and his contributions to

our constitutional government were based upon this re-
search. Jefferson maintained that "the experience of other
times and other nations" could provide the means for judging the future. According to Jefferson the people themselves were the only dependable safeguard against efforts
to subvert our constitutional government and what has
been called the revolution of 1800 demonstrated the point.
In this year the people voted the Federalists out of office,
voted against the centralization of government, voted
against the Alien and Sedition Bills and against open violations of the Bill of Rights. This revolt against the Federalist Party recalls Joseph Priestley's belief that great masses
of people can only be moved into action by great abuses
and, when they are so moved, they are always in the right.
There have been many violent precedents for this in history including the American Revolution, but Jefferson envisioned a system in which abuses of authority might be
challenged by the popular franchise. The practicality of
this idea was demonstrated for the first time in 1800. Since
then gross abuses of power have been checked again and
again by the American people in a reoccurring celebration
of the fact that this strangely co-ordinated system of *government by the people* was still working. The most immediate example of this is to be seen in the effective reaction of
the American people to Watergate. For the first time in our
political history a president was forced to resign because
of outraged public opinion.

The two party system was neither Federalist nor Republican according to Jefferson. The best government might
very well be the least government, but, in practice, political authority—and Jefferson did not except his own—in-

variably involved abuses of power. In a letter to Lafayette
in 1823 Jefferson stated:

> The Hartford Convention, the victory of Orleans, the
> peace of Ghent, prostrated the name of Federalism.
> Its votaries abandoned it through shame and mortifi-
> cation; and now call themselves Republicans. But the
> name alone is changed, the principles are the same.
> For in truth, the parties of Whig and Tory, are those
> of nature. They exist in all countries, whether called
> by these names or by those of Aristocrats and Demo-
> crats, Cote Droite and Cote Gauche, Ultras and Radi-
> cals, Serviles and Liberals.[1]

Whatever party name might be evoked, government of
the people rested squarely on the premise that the people
were capable of self-government and Jefferson was convinced that they were:

> I do not believe with the Rochefoucaults and Mon-
> taignes, that fourteen out of fifteen men are rogues:
> I believe a great abatement from that proportion may
> be made in favor of general honesty. But I have al-
> ways found that rogues would be uppermost, and I
> do not know that the proportion is too strong for the
> higher orders . . . These rogues set out with stealing
> the people's good opinion, and then steal from them
> the right of withdrawing it, by contriving laws and
> associations against the power of the people them-
> selves.[2]

Apparently these "associations" included whole schools
of writers and scholars. Their violent denunciations of
Jefferson for more than a century suggest their own inade-
quacy rather than Jefferson's. The novelist Gertrude Ather-

ton characterized Jefferson in the following passage from *The Conqueror*:

> The plebianism of his father showed itself in the ungainly shell, in the indifference to personal cleanliness, and in the mongrel spirit which drove him to acts of physical cowardice for which his apologists blush.[3]

This was supposed to be a description of the man who was to represent the young Republic in the court of Louis XVI and who came to be regarded as the most popular ambassador at that court. The Marquis de Lafayette in a letter to a friend in America, wrote: "No better minister could be sent to France. . . . He is everything that is good, upright, enlightened and clever, and is respected and beloved by every one that knows him."[4]

Theodore Roosevelt never disguised his contempt for Jefferson, describing him as a "scholarly, timid and shifting doctrinaire."[5] During his lifetime Jefferson was exposed to worse criticism and never answered it. He claimed that if he answered one libel he would immediately be confronted with twenty more. The poor opinions of Theodore Roosevelt or Gertrude Atherton might be brought into better perspective by comparing them with the statements of two men who knew Jefferson better than they did. John Adams describes Jefferson's appearance in 1775 as "Prompt, frank, explicit and decisive!" Lincoln in a letter written to H. L. Pierce and others in 1859 extends:

> All honor to Jefferson—the man who . . . had the coolness, forecast, and capacity to introduce into a merely revolutionary document, an abstract truth . . .

that today, and in all coming days, shall be a rebuke and a stumbling block to the very harbingers of reappearing tyranny and oppression.[6]

Recent history has confirmed one of Jefferson's most fundamental convictions. This "abstract truth," the unalienable right of the people to challenge all great matters of state policy at any time and by whatever means they may require. This natural right was not invented by Rousseau or discovered by John Locke or Joseph Priestley. Over a period of thousands of years it has simply surfaced again and again under the stress of tyrannical or inept abuses. Jefferson supposed that it was a moral right. In a letter to Dupont de Nemours in 1816 he says:

> But when we come to the moral principles on which government is to be administered, we come to what is proper for all conditions of society . . . Liberty, truth, probity, honor, are declared to be the four cardinal principles of your society. I believe with you that morality, compassion, generosity, are innate elements of the human constitution . . .[7]

Expressions of this kind were not naive. They were simply diverse elements in Jefferson's practical philosophy. His opinions of some individuals, on the venal press, or his belief that "every government degenerates when trusted to the rulers of the people alone" were in a most effective balance.

Jefferson had great predecessors in history who were not as practical. The Emperor Marcus Aurelius, a philosopher and a just man, was the first Roman emperor to systematically persecute the Christians. Jefferson shared his belief

in fundamental human decency with the Indian Emperor
Ashoka, a great ruler who became a convert to Buddhism.
Koppen has said that "If a man's fame can be measured
by the number of hearts who revere his memory, by the
number of lips who have mentioned, and still mention him
with honour, Ashoka is more famous than Charlemagne
or Caesar." This emperor would have readily understood
Jefferson's belief that morality, compassion and generosity
were innate in human nature. A modern translation of
Shankara's *Atmabodha* expresses the same thought:

> Every soul is divine, though during the state of ignor-
> ance it remains oblivious of its spiritual nature . . .
> Hence all men are entitled to respect. The divinity of
> the soul is the unshakable basis of democracy, self-
> determination, freedom, and other aspirations of
> modern minds.[8]

Occasional comments on religion appear in Jefferson's
letters but they generally refer to the Christian faith. John
Adams wrote a long letter to Jefferson in 1813 expressing
his high opinion of the Indian *Shastra* but this could not
have made much of an impression upon the classical schol-
ar who objected to Plato's obscurities. Ancient writers recommended by Jefferson included Xenophon, Epictetus,
Cicero, Seneca and Antonius. His own high morality was
a matter of inner conviction—perhaps it was innate. Jefferson's firm belief in the worth and dignity of human nature is the dominant theme in many of his letters and it is
most frequently expressed in political terms.

In 1784 Congress had authorized commercial treaties
with sixteen European states and in that same year Jeffer-

son was appointed Minister to France. For the next five years Jefferson's preoccupations with trade treaties were to be interrupted by the social life of Paris and finally by another Revolution.

Three distinguished Americans met at Passy, just outside Paris, on August 30, 1785. Franklin was 78 and in poor health. Jefferson, who was to replace him as Minister, held the old man in high esteem. John Adams reported six weeks later: "We proceed with wonderful harmony, good humor, and unanimity."

Jefferson must have found life in Paris quite interesting. This was a period when Montgolfier was planning the aerial navigation of the English Channel and Mesmer was presiding over his demonstrations of animal magnetism. Jefferson kept his friends in America informed of the invention of phosphorus matches, the cylinder lamp and the screw propeller. While negotiating for favored nation status to expand American trade in tobacco, whale oil and other commodities, Jefferson wrote *Observations on the Whale-Fishery,* a treatise on whaling and its historical importance.

Jefferson regarded France as a proper school for American patriots. In a letter to George Wythe in August 1786, Jefferson stated:

> If anybody thinks that kings, nobles, or priests are good conservators of the public happiness, send him here. It is the best school in the universe to cure him of that folly. He will see here, with his own eyes, that these descriptions of men are an abandoned confederacy against the happiness of the mass of the people.[9]

Jefferson was to remain in France for five years, long

enough to see the first eruptions of the French Revolution
and to be accused of being a Jacobin, an American Robespierre converted to "infidel doctrines." Very little evidence
of this has ever appeared. More plausibly Jefferson might
have been accused of indoctrinating the French aristocracy
with Americanism. While living in Paris he moved in a
select circle of society and was on friendly terms with
Madame d'Houdetot, the Comtesse de Tesse, Lafayette,
Condorcet, Cabanis, Madame Helvetius, Destutt de Tracy
and Du Pont de Nemours. The Marquis de Lafayette had
a copy of the Declaration of Independence hanging in his
study and he and his friends frequently conferred with
Jefferson at his home. On at least one occasion Jefferson
was seriously embarassed in his dual role as ambassador
and revolutionary authority. This hardly justified the
charges that he was a Jacobin. On the contrary, throughout his stay in Paris, Jefferson favored some sort of compromise with the monarchy and the more elemental
changes that were actually taking place were regarded as
unhappy exceptions to the rule. While in Paris, Jefferson
who had frequently proven his ability to accurately pre-
dict political changes, was in the position of a person not
able to see the woods for the trees. Most of his friends
were aristocrats and his view of the cataclysmic changes
that were taking place in the streets of Paris was almost
casual. In his autobiography Jefferson describes an inci-
dent that he witnessed personally:

> In the afternoon a body of about 100 German caval-
> ry were advanced and drawn up in the Place Louis
> XV. and about 200 Swiss posted at a little distance
> in their rear. This drew people to the spot, who thus

accidentally found themselves in front of the troops, merely at first as spectators; but as their numbers increased, their indignation rose. They retired a few steps, and posted themselves on and behind large piles of stones, large and small, collected in that Place for a bridge which was to be built adjacent to it. In this position, happening to be in my carriage on a visit, I passed through the lane they had formed, without interruption. But the moment after I had passed, the people attacked the cavalry with stones. They charged, but the advantageous position of the people, and the showers of stones obliged the horse to retire, and quit the field altogether, leaving one of their number on the ground, and the Swiss in their rear not moving to their aid. This was the signal for universal insurrection, and this body of cavalry, to avoid being massacred, retired toward Versailles. The people now armed themselves with such weapons as they could find in armorers' shops and private houses, and with bludgeons, and were roaming all night through all parts of the city, without any decided object.[10]

In 1789 seven princes of the blood royal and a variety of highly placed aristocrats and ex-ministers left France to escape the guillotine. On August 4th the Vicomte de Noailles made a motion to the Assembly to abolish all titles of rank and that body then proceeded with a systematic demolition of ancient abuses. A Constitutional Committee had been appointed in July to write a *Declaration of the Rights of Man* and the Assembly spent six weeks discussing the document. When Jefferson left France on the 9th of October he could not even have imagined the violence that was to follow the drafting of this French *Declaration.* On the other hand, he had already had his first intimations of a gathering storm in the United States. In a letter to William Stephens Smith dated Paris, February 2, 1788, Jefferson said:

It astonishes me to find such a change wrought in the opinions of our countrymen since I left them, as that three fourths of them should be contented to live under a system which leaves to their governors the power of taking from them the trial by jury in civil cases, freedom of religion, freedom of the press, freedom of commerce, the habeas corpus laws, and yoking them with a standing army. This is a degeneracy in the principles of liberty to which I had given four centuries instead of four years.[11]

This was not merely a political expression of Jefferson's interest in the adoption of a bill of rights. Jefferson's sensitive concern with the immediate future of the United States closely resembled that of a seer or clairvoyant, for his worst fears were to be fully realized in the course of the next ten years.

When Jefferson landed at Norfolk on November 23, 1789, he was informed of his nomination to the office of Secretary of State. He had sincerely wished to return to private life at Monticello but had, in effect, accepted President Washington's appointment when he wrote to the President saying: "You are to marshall us as may best be for the public good."

Jefferson took over his duties as Secretary of State in New York in March 1790 where he frequently conferred with President Washington, sometimes at the breakfast table. The entire staff of the Department of State consisted of two chief clerks, two assistants, and a part-time translator. Jefferson's intense pre-occupation with accumulations of official correspondence and documents was occasionally relieved by his cordial reception into New York society. Although politics was the most common subject of conversation on these occasions, Jefferson found himself in a minority of one in his defense of Republican principles. In a retrospective letter written to William Short in 1825, Jefferson refers to these dinner parties:

> When I arrived at New York in 1790, to take part in the administration, being fresh from the French revolution, while in its first and pure stage . . . I found a state of things, in the general society of the place, which I could not have supposed possible. Being a stranger there, I was feasted from table to table, at large set dinners, the parties generally from twenty to thirty. The revolution I had left, and that we had just gone through in the recent change of our own government, being the common topics of conversation. I was astonished to find the general prevalence of monarchial sentiments, insomuch that in maintaining those of Republicanism, I had always the whole company on my hands, never scarcely finding among them a single co-advocate in that argument, unless some old member of Congress happened to be present.[12]

When Jefferson first came to New York, he only knew Hamilton as Madison's collaborator in their exposition and defense of the Constitution in *The Federalist*. Not many weeks passed before Hamilton asked for Jefferson's support in a financial scheme which involved $20,000,000 of the states' debts. This was Jefferson's first regrettable encounter with the man who was to become his most formidable political enemy. In the following years Jefferson did not underestimate the man. Within a year Jefferson was to write in the *Anas*: "Hamilton was not only a monarchist but for a monarchy bottomed on corruption," and in a letter to James Madison in 1795 he warned:

> Hamilton is really a colossus to the anti-Republican party. Without numbers he is a host within himself. They have got themselves into a defile where they might be finished; but too much security on the Republican part will give time to his talents . . . In truth when he comes forward there is nobody but yourself who can meet him.[13]

With this characterization of Hamilton, Jefferson seems to have set the stage for an American form of the *No* drama. This ancient form of theatrical art sometimes dealt with human affairs. The cardinal virtues, fidelity, justice and charity, were personified. Multiple devils might appear and the play usually ended with some appropriate form of retribution. Washington, John Adams, Jefferson, Henry Knox, James Madison and Hamilton made up the cast. The play was to last for ten years ending dramatically in what was to be called the second American Revolution in 1800. Disagreements concerning the characterization in this American *No* drama are of little consequence for the play is repeated from time to time and the morality remains the same. Consider the devils and the men who conjured them. Between 1790 and 1800 wars against England, Tripoli, France and Spain were in process of being averted. The United States was being blackmailed by sovereign states located in Africa. State and Federal debts were being jobbed out at high rates of interest. Efforts to bolster up political uneasiness of one kind or another inspired officials to open the mail of private citizens. An extensive surveillance of American citizens was suggested by the executive and carried out by the Customs Service. The Alien and Sedition Laws were passed by Congress and editors were imprisoned for exercising their constitutional rights.

The first semblance of the cabinet appeared at the end of 1791 when President Washington felt the need to consult with his department heads. Indian affairs were the immediate issues under consideration. By December 15 negotiations with the new British minister, George Hammond, initiated a long series of statements, counterstatements, and curious evasions on the part of the British ambassador. Jefferson's relationship with Hamilton during this period was portrayed by the phrase, "Like two cocks in a pit."

Hammond had been instructed to negotiate articles of the treaty on unpaid debts and Loyalist property in return for leaving the Northwest posts. An American "assignment of breaches" was presented to Hammond by Jefferson. Hamilton violently opposed Jefferson's proposals observing that it was more important "to have the posts than to start a commercial war." English authorities charged the United States with a wanton violation of the treaty, with grave injuries to British subjects carefully detailed in five appendices. Two months later Jefferson answered the ninety-four charges made by the British government in a diplomatic note of 250 manuscript pages.

While in the cabinet, Jefferson and Hamilton had formed parties around them. Jefferson's partisanship had never wavered by a hair's breadth from the pure Republicanism he had expounded throughout his adult life. His opinions of the Secretary of the Treasury were no more flattering than Hamilton's were of Jefferson. However, Jefferson's opinions did have the quality of being more precise and probing. This appears clearly in a letter to Washington in 1792:

> That I have utterly in my private conversations disapproved of the system of the Secretary of the Treasury, Alexander Hamilton, I acknowledge and avow; and this was not a merely speculative difference. His system flowed from principles adverse to liberty and was calculated to undermine and demolish the republic, by creating an influence of his department over the members of the legislature. I saw this influence actually produced, and its first fruits to be the establishment of the great outlines of his project by the votes of the very persons who, having swallowed his bait, were laying themselves out to profit by his plans; and that had these persons withdrawn as those interested in a question ever should, the vote of the disinterested majority was clearly the reverse of what they made it. These were no longer then the votes of the representatives of the people, but of deserters from the rights and interests of the people.[14]

Jefferson had started writing his *Report on Commerce* in 1791. Based upon his ten years' experience negotiating trade treaties for the United States, it had been laid aside for many months before he made a decision to revise and expand it. It was read in the House on December 19 with somewhat spectacular effects for a paper on trade policies. The Secretary of State did not have an impressive record. No diplomatic triumphs marked the years of his office. The *Report on Commerce,* like others that he had made, was brilliantly written and formulated an aggressive opposition to what Hamilton called "my system." The Secretary of the Treasury said that Jefferson "threw this FIRE-BRAND of discord into the midst of the representatives . . . and instantly decamped to Monticello." Washington, who had hoped to establish a "coalition" government, accepted Jefferson's retirement with some reluctance.

Thomas Jefferson's hair was turning gray when he returned to Monticello. He was fifty years old and was looking forward to a career as a farmer and political innocent. But a gathering storm was already threatening the patriarch's retirement.

As early as 1795 Jefferson indicated the dangerous course that was being set by those whose sympathies for the British were as strong as Hamilton's. By this time the Federalists had come together as a war party. In a letter to James Monroe written on May 26, he declared:

> The servile copyist of Mr. Pitt, thought he too must have his alarms, his insurrections and plots against the Constitution. Hence the incredible fact that freedom of association, of conversation, and of the press, should in the 5th year of our government have been attacked under the form of a denunciation of the democratic societies, a measure which even England, as boldly as she is advancing to the establishment of an absolute monarchy has not yet been bold enough to attempt. Hence too the example of employing military force for civil purposes, when it has been impossible to produce a single fact of insurrection unless that term be entirely confounded with occasional riots . . . But it answered the favorite purposes of strengthening government and increasing public debt; and therefore an insurrection was announced and pro-

claimed and armed against, but could never be found.[15]

Matters more tangible than insurrections were envisioned by Jefferson in his famous letter to Phillip Mazzei. On April 24, 1796 he wrote:

> The aspect of our politics has wonderfully changed since you left us. In place of that noble love of liberty and republican government which carried us through the war, an Anglican, monarchial and aristocratical party has sprung up, whose avowed object is to draw over us the substance, as they have already done the forms, of the British Government. The main body of our citizens, however, remain true to their republican principles; the whole landed interest is republican, and so is a great mass of talents. Against us are the Executive, the Judiciary . . . . all the officers of the government, all who want to be officers, all timid men . . .[16]

The immediate wave of criticism which followed the publication of this letter had nothing to do with its accuracy. Jefferson's appraisal of Federalist sentiment was fairly justified, and within four years the American people proved that they were still loyally Republican.

The grand strategy of Hamilton and his party included a war with France, an alliance with Britain and a joint conquest of the Spanish colonies. While these Federalist schemes were taking shape the Venezuelan revolutionist Francesco Miranda sent an emissary to Philadelphia seeking this country's support for a South American revolution. John Adams would have nothing to do with these plans but wished to maintain the "possibility" of war with

France to build up American naval power. Hamilton, with the aid of the British Minister, hoped to bring about an alliance with England directed against France and Spain with Miranda as one of their pawns. The audacity of the Federalists' plans included a domestic use of the military and their unremitting attacks on Jefferson and his party were justified as attacks against Jacobins, enemy aliens and traitors. The passage of the Alien and Sedition Laws in 1798 was to be a direct implementation of Hamilton's grand strategy. Jefferson supposed that the first and second measures were directed against his close friend Volney. Volney and a substantial number of French nationals had already chartered a ship and left for France before the enactment of the Alien Law. Writing to James Madison earlier in the year, Jefferson had observed:

> At present, the war hawks talk of septembrizing, deportation and the examples set by the French executive. All the firmness of the human mind is now in a state of requisition.[17]

Jefferson's firmness was extraordinary. The Federalists intended to terrorize the opposition and the abuse of Jefferson reached an apocalyptic tempo. Logan, Bache and Jefferson were branded as American Jacobins and accused of a "traitorous conspiracy" in Congress. The *Porcupine's Gazette* warned the citizens of Philadelphia against these incendiaries, "fire is in your houses and the *couteau* at your throats." Prosecutions would seem to be in order.

Although Jefferson was insulted and lampooned from day to day he remained silent because of his official position. The Vice President was obliged to listen to the reading of a bill that he detested and could not defend himself against the most absurd libels. The personal abuse of his political enemies he ignored. Federalist attacks on the Constitution were carefully taken into account in his correspondence and a day of reckoning set—quite accurately—in the not distant future.

The Alien and Sedition Laws were signed by John Adams on July 14, 1798. Republicans declared that the States would not submit to such legislation and predicted that one of the first effects would be disaffection, violent opposition, tumults and recourse to the first revolutionary principles. The dangerous aliens described under the Alien Law had already left the country. The Sedition Law, however, could be enforced and it was. Twenty-five American citizens were arrested for violations of this law, fourteen were indicted and ten went to trial and were convicted. The fact that the fourteen were all Republican printers or publicists was certainly not a matter of chance. Prosecutions had begun in Massachusetts and no one in the country appeared to be safe under the Federalist terror.

In a letter to John Taylor on November 26, 1798, in which Jefferson says that his mail was tampered with, he outlines his idea of a proper procedure against the Sedition Law:

I owe you a political letter. Yet the infidelities of the post office and the circumstances of the times are against my writing fully and freely, whilst my own dispositions are as much against mysteries, innuendos and half confidences. I know not which mortifies me most, that I should fear to write what I think, or that my country bear such a state of things . . . We agree in all the essential ideas of your letter. We agree particularly in the necessity of some reform, and of some better security for civil liberty . . . For the present, I should be for resolving the alien and sedition laws to be against the constitution and merely void, and for addressing the other States to obtain similar declarations . . . It is a singular phenomenon, that while our State governments are the very *best in the world,* without exception or comparison, our general government has, in the rapid course of 9 or 10 years, become more arbitrary, and has swallowed more of the public liberty than even that of England.[18]

As the Sedition Law was a very real threat to Jefferson himself—he was the only highly placed official not given immunity under it—his cool reaction to it was surprising. Jefferson believed that authorized processes of law and the elective franchise would check this violation of constitutional authority by the Federalists and in the next two years his confidence in the American people was completely justified. Jefferson felt that while the northern States, particularly Massachusetts and Connecticut, dominated the situation it would be better to endure a very disagreeable situation than to threaten new regional controversies.

In a letter written to Edmund Pendleton on February 14, 1799, Jefferson pointed out that:

The violations of the constitution, propensities to war, to expense, and to a particular foreign connection, which we have lately seen, are becoming evident to the people, and are dispelling that mist which X. Y. Z. had spread before their eyes . . . New York and New Jersey are also getting into great agitation. In this State, (Pennsylvania) we fear that ill designing may produce insurrection. Nothing could be so fatal. Anything like force would check the progress of the public opinion and rally them around the goverment. This is not the kind of opposition the American people will permit. But keep away all show of force, and they will bear down the evil propensities of the government, by the constitutional means of election and petition. If we can keep quiet, therefore, the tide now turning will take a steady and proper direction. Even in N. Hampshire there are strong symptoms of a rising inquietude. In this state of things my dear Sir, it is more in your power than any other man's in the U. S. to give the *coup de grace* to the ruinous principles and practices we have seen.[19]

The German counties of York and Lancaster, which were normally Federalist, presented petitions signed by 4,000 irate citizens protesting the Alien and Sedition Laws. Citizens in New York and New Jersey were deeply agitated. Jefferson and Madison had prepared the Kentucky and Virginia resolutions as a protest against Federalist violations of the Constitution. The resolutions launched an attack against those who wished "to silence by force and not by reason the complaints or criticisms, just or unjust, of our citizens against the conduct of our agents." Petitions for repeal poured into Congress. The tide was turning as Jefferson had predicted it would. In 1799 the Federalists had a very substantial majority in Congress but their mandate was running out. Political history was being made and for the first time in this country a political party had engineered its own destruction. The Federalists knew that the Republican machine was greatly improved and that their agents were feverishly active in every part of the country. They were even more poignantly aware that the people in their own states had been thoroughly disillusioned by their conspiratorial tactics.

The Federalist Senator James Ross, who had been defeated in his own campaign for governor of Pennsylvania, and with the coming election in mind, moved the appointment of a committee to report a bill. The Ross bill provided that electoral certificates of the various states should be referred to a grand committee of six elected members from each house and the Chief Justice. They were to meet in secret session to examine the votes and throw out any they considered irregular. As the committee would be dominated by Federalists it could be expected to examine the Republican ballots very carefully.

William Doane, editor of the *Aurora,* heard of the plan and published the entire bill before it was voted on by the Senate. The editor of the *Aurora* had already been twice arraigned under the Sedition Law without a conviction. On the second attempt, a threat of embarrassing disclosures discouraged his prosecution. Summoned before Congress on charges of publishing false, scandalous, and malicious libel of the Senate, Doane once again proved himself too wily a prey for the Federalists. A series of delaying actions and postponements resulted in the Senate issuing a warrant for Doane's arrest. He had finally refused even to appear. At this point the editor went into hiding for a short time, but was again indicted in the fall and once again without success. This absurd exhibition of Federalist arrogance resulted in the defeat of the Ross bill. As the time for the election drew nearer, Federalist leaders continued their harrassing tactics. Enforcement of the Sedition

Law was pursued more vigorously than ever in an effort to silence the Republican press.

While the Federalists had been engaged in the most ferocious campaign of slander and vilification, Jefferson had been making a careful study of issues and men. As early as January 1789, Jefferson had outlined these campaign issues in a letter to Edmund Pendleton:

> If the understanding of the people could be rallied to the truth on this subject by exposing the dupery practiced on them, there are so many other things about to bear on them favorably . . . a reduction of the administration to constitutional principles cannot fail to be the effect. These are the Alien and Sedition Laws; the vexations of the Stamp Act; the disgusting particularities of the direct tax; the additional army without an enemy . . . a navy of fifty ships; five millions to be raised to build it on the usurious interest of eight per cent . . .[20]

Pamphlets attacking Jefferson as "an atheist" and as a "French infidel" exhibited a want of respect—not so much for Jefferson—as for the people themselves and some of the evidence for this was already in. The New York State election was an early triumph for the Republicans. The Republican ticket included several men who had become famous during the Revolution and the Federalists were decisively defeated. Jefferson supposed that the New York electoral vote would assure his election.

During the first months of the new century, it was quite evident that the Federalists were themselves divided and that the election of a Republican President was practically determined. In May Jefferson was nominated unanimously by the Republican Party for President and Aaron Burr was chosen to run for Vice-President. Jefferson spent the summer very quietly in Virginia. Between May and November he wrote only three letters.

The election took place early in November, but a month passed before the results were known. The Republican victory was marked by some apprehension as the votes in the Electoral College were evenly divided between Jefferson and Burr and this technicality inspired the Federalists to offer their support to Burr for the Presidency. A Federalist caucus was held in the House of Representatives and a majority of the party pledged its support to Burr in spite of bitter opposition on the part of Hamilton. It is a matter eternally to his credit that Alexander Hamilton refused to countenance a scheme to defeat the will of the people. Hamilton wrote to Wolcott:

> There is no doubt that upon every virtuous and prudent calculation, Jefferson is to be preferred. He is by far not so dangerous a man; and he has pretensions to character. As to Burr, there is nothing in his favor . . . He is truly the Cataline of America.[21]

The procedure to be followed in case of a tie in the electoral vote was for the House to ballot every hour without interruption of any other business until the tie was broken. Balloting started on February 11th and continued until February 19th. The efforts of some of the Federalists to gain concessions from Jefferson in return for their votes were consistently rejected. The character of this political Donnybrook in which an open usurpation of constitutional authority was contemplated by some members of the

House is clearly stated in a letter written by Jefferson to Monroe on February 15th:

> If they could have been permitted to pass a law for putting the government into the hands of an officer, they would certainly have prevented an election. But we thought it best to declare openly and firmly, one and all, that the day such an act passed, the Middle States would arm, and that no such usurpation, even for a single day, should be submitted to. This first shook them, and they were completely alarmed at the resource for which we declared, to wit, a convention to reorganize the government and to amend it. The very word convention gives them the horrors, as in the present democratical spirit of America, they fear they should lose some of the favorite morsels of the Constitution. Many attempts have been made to obtain terms and promises from me. I have declared to them, unequivocally, that I would not receive the government on capitulation, that I would not go into it with my hands tied.[22]

Jefferson was declared duly elected President after the 36th ballot.

When Thomas Jefferson came to Washington for his inaugural the city was made up of the scattered residences of a few thousand people, a "sprawling vastness between Georgetown and Anacostia." The Capitol and the President's House stood apart from these settlements with a magnificent view of the Potomac, virgin forests and distant heights. The shops of shoemakers, printers and tailors and a number of boarding houses clustered around the Capitol.

On the day of his inaugural Jefferson, according to an eyewitness, came from his own lodgings to the Capitol "on foot in his ordinary dress, escorted by a body of militia artillery from the neighboring State, and accompanied by the Secretaries of the Navy and the Treasury and a number of his political friends in the House of Representatives." The inaugural ceremonies were held in the Senate Chamber and Jefferson's address was conciliatory. Differences of opinion Jefferson asserted were "not a difference of principle."

> We have called, by different names, brethren of the same principle. We are all republicans: we are all federalists.
> If there be any among us who wish to dissolve this union, or to change its republican form, let them stand undisturbed, as monuments of the safety with which error of opinion may be tolerated where reason is left free to combat it.
> I know indeed that some honest men have feared that a republican government cannot be strong . . . I believe this, on the contrary, the strongest government on earth.

Jefferson carefully reviewed Republican principles:

> Equal and exact justice to all men, of whatever state or persuasion, religious or political:
> The diffusion of information, and arraignment of all abuses at the bar of the public reason;
> Freedom of Religion, freedom of the press, and freedom of Person under the protection of the Habeas corpus; And trial by juries, impartially selected.

Before concluding his address, Jefferson made—what his administration was to prove to be—a plain statement of his feelings and intentions:

The approbation implied by your suffrage, is a great consolation to me for the past; and my future solicitude will be to retain the good opinion of those who have bestowed it in advance, to conciliate that of others, by doing them all the good in my power, and to be instrumental to the happiness and freedom of all.[23]

When Jefferson moved into Washington in May he thought of the capital as almost pleasantly rural. The White House was in a much more satisfactory condition than in the autumn of 1800 when Mrs. Adams observed that it was "habitable" but unfinished. Jefferson wrote:

This may be considered as a pleasant country residence with a number of neat little villages scattered around within a distance of a mile and a half and furnishing a plain and substantially good society. They have begun their buildings in about four or five different points, and at each of which there are buildings enough to be considered as a village. The whole population is about six thousand.[24]

The reaction to Jefferson's inaugural address was extraordinary. His enigmatic sentences: "We are all republicans. We are all federalists." seems to have had the effect of a Cabalistic formula. Many Federalists including Henry Knox and Chief Justice Marshall reacted to it as though it were a victory speech by a member of their own party. A Federalist editor confessed:

We thought him a philosophist, and have found him a virtuous and enlightened philanthropist—We thought him a Virginian, and have found him an American—We thought him a partisan and have found him a president.[25]

The initiation of the "spoils system" has been attributed to Jefferson. The examples set by the Federalists before Jefferson became President makes this questionable. There was no scarcity of Federalists in political office under John Adams who even appointed Marshall Chief Justice after Jefferson's election. Jefferson did insist on appointing Republicans to new offices "until something like an equilibrium in office be restored." He was just as firm in refusing to dismiss Federalists who were competent.

The Republicans had a majority in both Houses when Congress met in December. The fact that Jefferson had the support of many Federalists, as well, gave him political advantages enjoyed by no other President in our history except Washington. Jefferson did not make the usual address to Congress, but sent written messages to both Houses declaring his intention to avoid formalities which tended to exalt an executive above private citizens. He expressed his particular concern with domestic affairs. He advocated economy in all public expenditures and this included a thorough review of the Civil Service, the Army and the Navy. Congress was in complete sympathy with these proposals. A recommendation to permit newspaper reporters to attend the sessions of both Houses became a partisan issue but was passed anyway.

Sometime before Congress adjourned in May, the President's preoccupation with domestic affairs was sharply diverted by the news that Spain had ceded Florida and Louisiana back to France. Madison was at once requested to draw up instructions for the American Minister to France. These were to be based upon the expected economic and political results of this retrocession and were

to include securing just and permanent rights of navigation of the Mississippi and the acquirement of the island
of New Orleans. Jefferson supposed that Spain might have
held this territory indefinitely but that France was too
dangerous for a neighbor. In a letter to Robert Livingston
in Paris, Jefferson appeared to be completely uninhibited
politically. With his own country's interests at stake, this
long time friend of the French, the American Robespierre,
was quite capable of threatening Napoleon with an American alliance with Britain:

> The day that France takes possesion of N. Orleans
> fixes the sentence which is to restrain her forever with-
> in her low water mark. It seals the union of two na-
> tions who in conjunction can maintain exclusive pos-
> session of the ocean. From that moment we must
> marry ourselves to the British fleet and nation ... and
> having formed and cemented together a power which
> may render reinforcement of her settlements here
> impossible to France, make the first cannon, which
> shall be fired in Europe the signal for tearing up any
> settlement she may have made, and for holding the
> two continents of America in sequestration for the
> common purposes of the united British and American
> nations.[26]

Jefferson's allusion to a naval alliance with the British was
not an empty threat. The Abbe Sieyes said that Napoleon
was the man who "knows everything, wants everything,
and can do everything," and no one at that time was inclined to question his mastery of Europe. Napoleon's star,
however, had already started setting in the west. He had
dreamed of colonizing the new world for some time, expeditions had been planned, but a revolt of black slaves

in Santo Domingo had become a serious obstacle to his plans. Napoleon's brother-in-law General LeClerc had been sent to Santo Domingo to quell these disorders. This expedition had been organized on a grand scale. Leclerc had 50,000 French troops under his command before his own death and the remnant of this force was driven into the sea by the black revolutionists. Napoleon had many plans . . . and at St. Cloud on April 11, 1803, he declared "Irresolution and deliberation are no longer in season, I renounce Louisiana."[27]

In the months that followed the price of Louisiana was finally set at $15,000,000 and the treaty was signed. On this occasion Robert Livingston proudly stated: "From this day the United States take their place among the powers of the first rank." The territory of Louisiana was a howling wilderness as some Federalists suggested, but it more than doubled the land area of this country and its acquisition was one of the most important single acts of government in our history. Certainly it was the crowning achievement in Thomas Jefferson's career.

When Jefferson became President in 1801 many Europeans regarded our society as some kind of compromise between barbarism and anarchy. This was in curious contrast with the facts. From a national capital that was little more than a village, issues and established procedures were being projected to the ends of the earth. In 1801 the people of this nation, numbering some four millions, were the government, and their representatives were negotiating with the Tzar of Russia, the pirates of Tripoli, Napoleon, and the government of His British Majesty, with great authority.

The Declaration of Independence was derived from many sources. Its great originality was that it gave direct expression to the thoughts and feelings of millions of Americans.

The Rights of Man

To Henry Lee. Monticello, May 8, 1825.

Dear Sir—. . . That George Mason was the author of the bill of rights, and of the constitution founded on it, the evidence of the day established fully in my mind. Of the paper you mention, purporting to be instructions to the Virginia delegation in Congress, I have no recollection. . . . But with respect to our rights, and the acts of the British government contravening those rights, there was but one opinion on this side of the water. All American whigs thought alike on these subjects. When forced, therefore, to resort to arms for redress, an appeal to the tribunal of the world was deemed proper for our justification. This was the object of the Declaration of Independence. Not to find out new principles, or new arguments, never before thought of, not merely to say things which had never been said before; but to place before mankind the common sense of the subject, in terms so plain and firm as to command their assent, and to justify ourselves in the independent stand we are compelled to take. Neither aiming at originality of principle or sentiment, nor yet copied from any particular and previous writing, it was intended to be an expression of the American mind, and to give to that expression the proper tone and spirit called for by the occasion. All its authority rests then on the harmonizing sentiments of the day, whether expressed in conversation, in letters, printed essays, or in the elementary books of public right, as Aristotle, Cicero, Locke, Sidney, etc.[1]

To John Adams. 1813.

Men have differed in opinion, and been divided into parties by these opinions, from the first origin of societies, and in all governments where they have been permitted freely to think and to speak. The same political parties which now agitate the United States have existed through all time. Whether the power of the people or that of the tyrant should prevail, were questions which kept the States of Greece and Rome in eternal convulsions, as they now schismatize every people whose minds and mouths are not shut up by the gag of a despot. And, in fact, the terms of Whig and Tory belong to natural as well as to civil history. They denote the temper and constitution of the mind of different individuals. To come to our own country and to the time when you and I became first acquainted, we will remember the violent parties which agitated the old Congress, and their contents. There you and I were together, and the Jays, and the Dickinsons, and other anti-independents, were arrayed against us. They cherished the monarchy of England, and we the rights of our countrymen. When our present government was passing from Confederation to Union, how bitter was the schism between the Feds and the Antis. Here you and I were together again. For, although for a moment separated by the Atlantic from the scene of action, I favored the opinion that nine States should confirm the Constitution, in order to secure it, and the others hold off until certain amendments, deemed favorable to freedom should be made. I rallied in the first instant to the wiser proposition of Massachusetts, that all should confirm, and then all instruct their delegates to urge those amendments. The amendments were made, and all were reconciled to the government. But as soon as it was put into motion, the line of division was again drawn. We broke into two parties, each wishing to give the government a different direction; the one to strengthen the most popular branch, the other the more permanent branches, and to extend their permanence. . . . There have been differences of opinion and party differences, from the first establishment of governments to the present day, and on the same question which now divides our own country; that these will continue through all future time; that everyone takes his side in favor of the many, or of the few, according to constitution, and the circumstances in which he is placed . . .[2]

To Monsieur A. Coray. Monticello, October 31, 1823.

The government of Athens, for example, was that of the people of one city making laws for the whole country subjected to them. That of Lacedaemon was the rule of military monks over the laboring class of the people, reduced to abject slavery. These are not the doctrines of the present age. The equal rights of man, and the happiness of every individual, are now acknowledged to be the only legitimate objects of government. Modern times have the signal advantage, too, of having discovered the only device by which these rights can be secured, to wit: government by the people, acting not in person, but by representatives chosen by themselves, that is to say, by every man of ripe years and sane mind, who either contributes by his purse or person to the support of his country. The small and imperfect mixture of representative government in England, impeded as it is by other branches, aristocratical and hereditary, shows yet the power of the representative principle towards improving the condition of man. With us, all the branches of the government are elective by the people themselves, except the judiciary, of whose science and qualifications they are not competent judges. Yet, even in that department, we call in a jury of the people to decide all controverted matters of fact, because to that investigation they are entirely competent, leaving thus as little as possible, merely the law of the case, to the decision of the judges. And true it is that the people, especially when moderately instructed, are the only safe, because the only honest, depositories of the public rights, and should therefore be introduced into the administration of them in every function to which they are sufficient; they will err sometimes and accidentally, but never designedly, and with a systematic and persevering purpose of overthrowing the free principles of the government. Hereditary bodies, on the contrary, always existing, always on the watch for their own aggrandizement, profit of every opportunity of advancing the privileges of their order, and encroaching on the rights of the people.[3]

To Mrs. John Adams. Monticello, September 11, 1804.

I tolerate with the utmost latitude the right of others to differ from me in opinion without imputing to them criminality. I know too well the weakness and uncertainty of human reason to wonder at its different results. Both of our political parties, at least the honest part of them, agree conscientiously in the same object—the public good; but they differ essentially in what they deem the means of promoting that good. One side believes it best done by one composition of the governing powers; the other, by a different one. One fears most the ignorance of the people; the other, the selfishness of rulers independent of them. Which is right, time and experience will prove.[4]

To Francis Hopkinson. 1789.

I am not a Federalist, because I never submitted the whole system of my opinions to the creed of any party of men whatever, in religion, in philosophy, in politics, or in anything else where I was capable of thinking for myself. Such an addiction is the last degradation of a free and moral agent. If I could not go to heaven but with a party, I would not go there at all.[5]

To Joel Barlow. 1802.

We shall now be so strong that we shall certainly split again; for freemen thinking differently and speaking and acting as they think, will form into classes of sentiment, but it must be under another name; that of Federalism is to become so scanted that no party can rise under it. As the division between Whig and Tory is founded in the nature of men, the weakly and nerveless, the rich and the corrupt, seeing more safety and accessibility in a strong executive; the healthy, firm and virtuous feeling confidence in their physical and moral resources and willing to part with only so much power as is necessary for their good government, and therefore to retain the rest in the hands of the many, the division will substantially be into Whig and Tory, as in England, formerly.[6]

To Mr. A. Donald. Paris, February 7, 1788.

I wish with all my soul, that the nine first conventions may accept the new constitution, because this will secure to us the good it contains, which I think great and important. But I equally wish, that the four latest conventions, whichever they be, may refuse to accede to it, till a declaration of rights be annexed. This would probably command the offer of such a declaration, and thus give to the whole fabric, perhaps, as much perfection as any one of that kind ever had. By a declaration of rights, I mean one which shall stipulate freedom of religion, freedom of the press, freedom of commerce against monopolies, trial by juries in all cases, no suspensions of the habeas corpus, no standing armies. These are fetters against doing evil, which no honest government should decline.[7]

To Noah Webster. Philadelphia, December 4, 1790.

It had become an universal and almost uncontroverted position in the several States, that the purposes of society do not require a surrender of all our rights to our ordinary governors; that there are certain portions of right not necessary to enable them to carry on an effective government, and which experience has nevertheless proved they will be constantly encroaching on, if submitted to them; that there are also certain fences which experience has proved peculiarly efficacious against wrong, and rarely obstructive of right, which yet the governing powers have ever shown a disposition to weaken and remove. Of the first kind, for instance, is freedom of religion; of the second, trial by jury, habeas corpus laws, free presses. These were the settled opinions of all the States,—of that of Virginia, of which I was writing, as well as of the others. The others had, in consequence, delineated these unceded portions of right and these fences against wrong, which they meant to exempt from the power of their governors, in instruments called declarations of rights and constitutions; and as they did this by conventions, which they appointed for the express purpose of reserving these rights, and of delegating others to their ordinary legislative, executive, and judiciary bodies, none of the reserved rights can be touched without resorting to the people to appoint another convention for the express purpose of permitting it.[8]

To James Madison. Paris, December 20, 1787.

I like much the general idea of framing a government, which should go on of itself, peaceably, without needing continual recurrence to the State legislatures. I like the organization of the government into legislative, judiciary and executive. I like the power given to the legislature to levy taxes, and for that reason solely, I approve of the greater House being chosen by the people directly . . . I like the negative given to the Executive, conjointly with a third of either House; though I should have liked it better, had the judiciary been associated for that purpose, or invested separately with a similar power. There are other good things of less moment. I will now tell you what I do not like. First, the omission of a bill of rights, providing clearly, and without the aid of sophism, for freedom of religion, freedom of the press, protection against standing armies, restriction of monopolies, the eternal and unremitting force of the habeas corpus laws, and trials by jury in all matters of fact triable by the laws of the land, and not by the laws of nations . . . Let me add, that a bill of rights is what the people are entitled to against every government on earth, general or particular; and what no just government should refuse, or rest on inference.[9]

From Notes on Virginia. *1782.*

But of all the views of this law relating to popular education none is more important, none more legitimate, than that of rendering the people the safe, as they are the ultimate, guardians of their own liberties. For this purpose the reading in the first stage, where they will receive their whole education, is proposed to be chiefly historical. History, by apprising them of the past, will enable them to judge of the future; it will avail them of the experience of other times and other nations; it will qualify them as judges of the actions and designs of men; it will enable them to know ambition under every disguise it may assume; and knowing it to defeat its views.[10]

To John Adams. Monticello. October 28, 1813.

At the first session of our legislature after the Declaration of Independence, we passed a law abolishing entails. And this was followed by one abolishing the privilege of primogeniture, and dividing the lands of intestates equally among all their children, or other representatives. These laws, drawn by myself, laid the ax to the foot of pseudo-aristocracy. And had another which I prepared been adopted by the legislature, our work would have been complete. It was a bill for the more general diffusion of learning. This proposed to divide every county into wards of five or six miles square, like your townships; to establish in each ward a free school for reading, writing and common arithmetic; to provide for the annual selection of the best subjects from these schools, who might receive at the public expense, a higher degree of education at a district school; and from these district schools to select a certain number of the most promising subjects, to be completed at an University, where all the useful sciences should be taught. Worth and genius would thus have been sought out from every condition of life, and completely prepared by education for defeating the competition of wealth and birth for public trusts. My proposition had, for a further object, to impart to these wards those portions of self-government for which they are best qualified, by confiding to them the care of their poor, their roads, police, elections, the nomination of jurors, administration of justice in small cases, elementary exercises of militia; in short, to have made them little republics, with a warden at the head of each, for all those concerns which, being under their eye, they would better manage than the larger republics of the county or State. A general call of ward meetings by their wardens on the same day through the State would at any time produce the genuine sense of the people on any required point, and would enable the State to act in mass, as your people have so often done, and with so much effect by their town meetings. The law for religious freedom, which made a part of this system, having put down the aristocracy of the clergy, and restored to the citizen the freedom of the mind, and those of entails and descents nurturing an equality of condition among them, this on education would have raised the mass of the people to the high ground of moral respectability necessary to their own safety, and to orderly government . . . Although this law has not yet been acted on but in a small and inefficient degree, it is still considered as before the legislature, with other bills of the revised code, not yet taken up, and I have great hope that some patriotic spirit will, at a favorable moment, call it up, and make it the key-stone of the arch of our government.[11]

When Jefferson was appointed Minister to France in 1785 he was placed in a most advantageous position to observe the second great revolution of the eighteenth century. His personal experiences and conclusions are mentioned in many of his letters and he found France "the best school in the world" in which to study the follies of monarchical government.

Minister to France

To George Wythe. Paris, 1786.

If all the sovereigns of Europe were to set themselves to work, to emancipate the minds of their subjects from their present ignorance and prejudices, and that, as zealously as they now endeavor the contrary, a thousand years would not place them on the high ground, on which our common people are now setting out. Ours could not have been so fairly placed under the control of the common sense of the people, had they not been separated from their parent stock, and kept from contamination, either from them, or the other people of the old world, by the intervention of so wide an ocean. To know the worth of this, one must see the want of it here. I think by the far the most important bill in our whole code, is that for the diffusion of knowledge among the people. No other sure foundation can be devised, for the preservation of freedom and happiness. If anybody thinks that kings, nobles, or priests are good conservators of the public happiness, send him here. It is the best school in the universe to cure him of that folly. He will see here, with his own eyes, that these descriptions of men are an abandoned confederacy against the happiness of the mass of the people . . . Preach, my dear Sir, a crusade against ignorance; establish and improve the law for educating the common people.[1]

To Mrs. Adams. July 7, 1785.

You see the value of energy in Government for such a measure, which would have wrapt in the flames of war and desolation in America, ends without creating the slightest disturbance. Every attempt to criticize even mildly the government is followed immediately by stern measures, suppressing the London papers, suppressing the *Leyden Gazette,* imprisoning Beaumarchais and imprisoning the editor of the *Journal,* the author of the *Mercure,* etc.[3]

To Rev. William Smith. 1791.

The succession to Dr. Franklin, at the court of France, was an excellent school of humility. On being represented to anyone as the Minister of America, the commonplace question used in such cases was *"C'est vous, Monsieur, qui remplace le Docteur Franklin;"* "It is you, Sir, who replace Dr. Franklin." I generally answered, "No one can replace him, Sir; I am only his successor."[4]

To Major General Greene. Paris, January 12, 1786.

Dear Sir, Your favor of June the 1st did not come to hand till the 3rd of September. I immediately made inquiries on the subject of the frigate you had authorized your relation to sell to this government, and I found that he had long before that sold her to the government, and sold her very well, as I understood. I noted the price on the back of your letter, which I have since unfortunately mislaid, so that I cannot at this moment state to you the price. But the transaction is of so long standing that you cannot fail to have received advice of it. I should without delay have given you this information, but that I hoped to be able to accompany it with information as to the live-oak, which

was another object of your letter. This matter, though it
has been constantly pressed by Mr. St. John, and also by
the Marquis de la Fayette, since his return from Berlin,
has been spun to a great length, and at last they have only
decided to send to you for samples of the wood. Letters
on this subject from the Marquis de la Fayette accompany
this.

Every thing in Europe is quiet, and promises quiet for
at least a year to come. We do not find it easy to make
commercial arrangements in Europe. There is a want of
confidence in us. This country has lately reduced the duties
on American whale-oil to about a guinea and a half the
ton, and I think they will take the greatest part of what
we can furnish. I hope, therefore, that this branch of our
commerce will resume its activity. Portugal shows a disposition to court our trade; but this has for some time been
discouraged by the hostilities of the piratical states of Bar-
bary. The Emperor of Morocco, who had taken one of our
vessels, immediately consented to suspend hostilities and
ultimately gave up the vessel, cargo, and crew. I think we
shall be able to settle matters with him. But I am not
sanguine as to the Algerines. They have taken two of our
vessels, and I fear will ask such a tribute for a forbearance
of their piracies as the United States would be unwilling to
pay. When this idea comes across my mind, my faculties
are absolutely suspended between indignation and impa-
tience. I think whatever sums we are obliged to pay for
freedom of navigation in the European seas, should be
levied on the European commerce with us by a separate
impost, that these powers may see that they protect these
enormities for their own loss.[5]

To Mr. Wythe. Paris, August 13, 1786.

The European papers have announced, that the Assembly of Virginia were occupied on the revisal of their code of laws. This, with some other similar intelligence, has contributed much to convince the people of Europe, that what the English papers are constantly publishing of our anarchy, is false; as they are sensible that such a work is that of a people only, who are in perfect tranquility. Our act for freedom of religion is extremely applauded.[6]

To Stephens Smith. Paris, 1787.

The British ministry have so long hired their gazetteers to repeat and model into every form lies about our being in anarchy, that the world has at length believed them, the ministers themselves have come to believe them, and what is more wonderful we have believed them ourselves. Yet where does the anarchy exist? When did it ever exist except in the single instance of Massachusetts?[7]

To James Monroe. Paris. August 28, 1785.

The English papers so incessantly repeating their lies about the tumults, the anarchy, the bankruptcies and distresses of America, these ideas prevail generally in Europe. At a large table where I dined the other day, a gentleman from Switzerland expressed his apprehensions for the fate of Dr. Franklin as he said he had been informed he would be received with stones by the people, who were generally dissatisfied with the revolution and incensed against all those who had assisted in bringing it about. I told him his apprehensions were just, and that the People of America would probably salute Dr. Franklin with the same stones they had thrown at the Marquis Fayette. The reception of the Doctor is an object of very general attention, and will weigh in Europe as an evidence of the satisfaction or dissatisfaction of America with their revolution.[8]

To William Stephens Smith. Paris, February 2, 1788.

I am glad to learn by letters which come down to the 20th of December that the new constitution will undoubtedly be received by a sufficiency of the States to set it going. Were I in America, I would advocate it warmly till nine should have adopted and then as warmly take the other side to convince the remaining four that they ought not to come into it till the declaration of rights is annexed to it. By this means we should secure all the good of it, and procure so respectable an opposition as would induce the accepting states to offer a bill of rights. This would be the happiest turn the thing could take. I fear much the effects of the perpetual re-eligibility of the President. But it is not thought of in America, and have therefore no prospect of a change of that article. But I own it astonishes me to find such a change wrought in the opinions of our countrymen since I left them, as that three fourths of them should be contented to live under a system which leaves to their governors the power of taking from them the trial by jury in civil cases, freedom of religion, freedom of the press, freedom of commerce, the habeas corpus laws, and yoking them with a standing army. This is a degeneracy in the principles of liberty to which I had given four centuries instead of four years. But I hope it will all come about. We are now vibrating between too much and too little government, and the pendulum will rest finally in the middle.[9]

To James Madison. Paris, August 28, 1789.

The tranquility of the city has not been disturbed since my last. Dissensions between the French and Swiss guards occasioned some private combats in which five or six were killed. These dissensions are made up. The want of bread for some days past has greatly endangered the peace of the city. Some get a little, some none at all. The poor are best served because they besiege perpetually the doors of the bakers. Notwithstanding this distress, and the palpable impotence of the city administration to furnish bread to the city, it was not till yesterday that general leave was given to the bakers to go into the country and buy flour for themselves as they can. This will soon relieve us, because the wheat harvest is well advanced. Never was there a country where the practice of governing too much had taken deeper root and done such mischief. Their declaration of rights is finished. If printed in time I will enclose a copy with this. It is doubtful whether they will now take up the finance or the constitution first. The distress for money endangers everything. No taxes are paid, and no money can be borrowed.[10]

To James Madison. Paris, July 31, 1788.

I send you also two little pamphlets of the Marquis de Condorcet, wherein is the most judicious statement I have seen of the great questions which agitate this nation at present. The new regulations present a preponderance of good over their evil but they suppose that the King can model the constitution at will, or in other words that his government is a pure despotism. The question then arising is whether a pure despotism in a single head, or one which is divided among a king, nobles, priesthood, and numerous magistracy is the least bad. I should be puzzled to decide: but I hope they will have neither, and that they are advancing to a limited, moderate government, in which the people will have a good share.[11]

To Benjamin Hawkins. Paris, August 4, 1787.

I look up with you to the Federal convention for an amendment of our federal affairs. Yet I do not view them in so disadvantageous a light at present as some do. And above all things I am astonished at some people's considering a kingly government as a refuge. Advise such to read the fable of the frogs who solicited Jupiter for a king. If that does not put them to rights, send them to Europe to see something of the trappings of monarchy, and I will undertake that every man shall go back thoroughly cured. If all the evils which can arise among us from the republican form of our government from this day to the day of judgement could be put into a scale against what this country suffers from its monarchial form in a week, or England in a month, the latter would preponderate. Consider the contents of the red book in England, or the Almanac royale of France, and say what a people gain by monarchy. No race of kings has ever presented above one man of common sense in twenty generations. The best they can do is to leave things to their ministers, and what are their ministers but a committee, badly chosen? If the king ever meddles it is to do harm.[12]

To M. L'Abbe Arnoud. Paris, July 19, 1789.

Dear Sir.—The annexed is a catalogue of all the books

I recollect on the subject of juries. With respect to the value of this institution, I must make a general observation. We think, in America, that it is necessary to introduce the people into every department of government, as far as they are capable of exercising it; and that this is the only way to insure a long-continued and honest administration of its powers.

1. They are not qualified to exercise themselves the executive department, but they are qualified to name the person who shall exercise it. With us, therefore, they choose this officer every four years.

2. They are not qualified to legislate. With us, therefore, they only choose the legislators.

3. They are not qualified to judge questions of *law,* but they are very capable of judging questions of *fact.* In the form of juries, therefore, they determine all matters of fact, leaving to the permanent judges, to decide the law resulting from those facts. But we all know that permanent judges acquire an *Esprit de corps*; that being known, they are liable to be tempted by bribery; that they are misled by favor, by relationship, by a spirit of party, by a devotion to the executive or legislative power; that it is better to leave a cause to the decision of cross and pile, than to that of a judge biased to one side; and that the opinion of twelve honest jurymen gives still a better hope of right, than cross and pile does. It is in the power, therefore, of the juries, if they think permanent judges are under any bias whatever, in any cause, to take on themselves to judge the law as well as the fact. They never exercise this power but when they suspect partiality in the judges; and by the exercise of this power, they have been the firmest

bulwarks of English liberty. Were I called upon to decide, whether the people had best be omitted in the legislative or judiciary department, I would say it is better to leave them out of the legislative. The execution of the laws is more important than the making of them. However, it is best to have the people in all the three departments, where that is possible.[13]

To Thomas Paine. Paris, July 11, 1789.

The *National Assembly,* then, (for that is the name they take,) having shown through every stage of these transactions a coolness, wisdom, and resolution to set fire to the four corners of the kingdom, and to perish with it themselves, rather than to relinquish an iota from their plan of a total change of government, are now in complete and undisputed possession of the sovereignty. The executive and aristocracy are at their feet; the mass of the nation, the mass of the clergy, and the army are with them: they have prostrated the old government, and are now beginning to build one from the foundation. A committee, charged with the arrangement of their business, gave in, two days ago, the following order of proceedings.

1. Every government should have for its only end, the preservation of the rights of man: whence it follows, that to recall constantly the government to the end proposed, the constitution should begin by a declaration of the natural and imprescriptible rights of man.

Declaration of the rights of man. Principles of the monarchy. Rights of the nation. Rights of the King. Rights of the citizens.

Organization and rights of the National Assembly. . . .

You see that these are the materials of a superb edifice, and the hands which have prepared them are perfectly capable of putting them together, and of filling up the work, of which these are only the outlines. While there are some men among them of very superior abilities, the mass possess such a degree of good sense, as enables them to decide well. I have always been afraid their numbers might lead to confusion. Twelve hundred men in one room are too many. I have still that fear. Another apprehension is, that a majority cannot be induced to adopt the trial by jury; and I consider that as the only anchor ever yet imagined by man, by which a government can be held to the principles of its constitution.[14]

To William Carmichael. Paris, 1789.

The revolution in this country seems to be going on well. . . . The circumstance from which I fear the worst is that the States General are too numerous. I see great difficulty in preventing 1,200 people from becoming a mob. Should confusion be prevented from this circumstance, I suppose the States General, with the consent of the King, will establish some of the leading features of a good constitution.[15]

To David Humphreys. Paris, 1789.

The change in this country since you left it is such as you can form no idea of. The frivolities of conversation have given way entirely to politics. Men, women, and children talk nothing else. The press groans with daily productions which in point of boldness make an Englishman stare. A complete revolution in this government has, within the space of two years been effected merely by the force of public opinion, aided indeed by the want of money which the dissipations of the court had brought on. The assembly of the States General begins the 27th of April. The representation of the people will be perfect. But they will be alloyed by an equal number of nobility and clergy. . . . I believe this nation will in the course of the present year have as full a portion of liberty dealt out to them as the nation can bear at present, considering how uninformed the mass of their people is.[16]

To Edward Rutledge, 1791.

I still hope the French revolution will issue happily. I feel that the permanence of our own leans in some degree on that, and that failure there would be a powerful argument to prove a failure here.[17]

To James Madison. 1792.

This ministry which is of the Jacobin party cannot but be favorable to us, as that whole party must be. Indeed notwithstanding the very general abuse of the Jacobins, I begin to consider them as representing the true revolution spirit of the whole nation, and as carrying the nation with them.[18]

To William Short. 1793.

I considered the Jacobins as the same with the Republican patriots and the Feuillants, as the monarchical patriots, well known in the early part of the Revolution and but little distant in their views, both having in object the establishment of a free constitution, and differing only on the question whether their chief Executor should be hereditary or not. The Jacobins (as since called) yielded to the Feuillants and tried the experiment of retaining their hereditary Executive. The experiment failed completely, and would have brought on the re-establishment of despotism had it been pursued. The Jacobins saw this, and that the expunging that officer was of absolute necessity. And the nation was with them in opinion.[19]

To Jedidiah Morse. 1822.

The society of Jacobins, in another country, was instituted on principles and views as virtuous as ever kindled the hearts of patriots. It was the pure patriotism of their purposes which extended their association to the limits of the nation, and rendered their power within it boundless; and it was this power which degenerated their principles and practices to such enormities as never before could have been imagined.[20]

To Mrs. John Adams. Paris, July 7, 1785.

Dear Madam, I had the honor of writing you on the 21st of June, but the letter being full of treason, has waited a private conveyance. Since that date there has been received for you at Auteuil a cask of about 60 gallons of wine. I would have examined its quality, and have ventured to decide on its disposal, but it is in a cask within a cask, and therefore cannot be got at but by operations which would muddy it and disguise its quality. As you probably know what it is, what it cost, etc., be so good as to give me your orders on the subject and they shall be complied with.

Since my last I can add another chapter to the history of the *redacteur* of the *Journal de Paris*. After the paper had been discontinued about three weeks it appeared again, but announcing in the first sentence a *changement de domicile* of the *redacteur,* the English of which, is that the redaction of the paper had been taken from the imprisoned culprit, and given to another. Whether the imprisonment of the former has been made to cease, or what will be the last chapter of his history I cannot tell. I love energy in Government dearly,—it is evident it has become necessary on this occasion, and that a very daring spirit has lately appeared in this country, for notwithstanding the several examples lately made of suppressing the London papers, suppressing the *Leyden Gazette,* imprisoning Beaumarchais, and imprisoning the redacteur of the *Journal* . . .

The settlement of the affairs of the Abbie Mably is likely to detain his friends Arnoud and Chault in Paris the greatest part of the summer. It is a fortunate circumstance for me, as I have much society, with them.—What mischief is this which is brewing anew between Faneuil hall and the nation of God-demmees? Will that focus of sedition be never extinguished? I apprehend the fire will take thro' all the states and involve us again in the displeasure of our Mother Country.[21]

To M. Destutt Tracy. Monticello, January 26, 1811.

One of its doctrines, indeed, the preference of a plural over a singular executive, will probably not be assented to here. When our present government was first established, we had many doubts on this question, and many leanings towards a supreme executive council. It happened that at that time the experiment of such an one was commenced in

France, while the single executive was under trial here. We watched the motions and effects of these two rival plans, with an interest and anxiety proportioned to the importance of a choice between them. The experiment in France failed after a short course, and not from any circumstance peculiar to the times or nation, but from those internal jealousies and dissensions in the Directory, which will ever arise among men equal in power, without a principal to decide and control their differences. We had tried a similar experiment in 1784, by establishing a committee of the States, composed of a member from every State, then thirteen, to exercise the executive functions during the recess of Congress. They fell immediately into schisms and dissensions, which became at length so inveterate as to render all co-operation among them impracticable: they dissolved themselves, abandoning the helm of government, and it continued without a head, until Congress met the ensuing winter. This was then imputed to the temper of two or three individuals; but the wise ascribed it to the nature of man. The failure of the French Directory, and from the same cause, seems to have authorized a belief that the form of a plurality, however promising in theory, is impracticable with men constituted with the ordinary passions. While the tranquil and steady tenor of our single executive, during a course of twenty-two years of the most tempestuous times the history of the world has ever presented, gives a rational hope that this important problem is at length solved. Aided by the counsels of a cabinet of Heads of departments, originally four, but now five, with whom the President consults, either singly or all together, he has the benefit of their wisdom and information, brings their views to one center, and produces an unity of action and direction in all the branches of government. The excellence of this construction of the executive power has already manifested itself here under very opposite circumstances. During the administration of our first President, his cabinet of four members was equally divided, by as marked an opposition of principle, as monarchism and republicanism could bring into conflict. Had that cabinet been a directory, like positive and negative quantities in Algebra, the opposing wills would have balanced each other, and produced a state of absolute inaction. But the President heard with calmness the opinions and reasons of each, decided the course to be pursued, and kept the government steadily in it, unaffected by the agitation. The public knew well the dissensions of the cabinet, but never had an uneasy thought on their account; because they knew also they had provided a regulating power, which would keep the machine in steady movement. I speak with an intimate knowledge of these scenes, *quorum pars fui*; as I may of others of a character entirely opposite. The third administration, which was of eight years, presented an example of harmony in a cabinet of six persons, to which perhaps history has furnished no parallel. There never arose, during the whole time, an instance of an unpleasant thought or word between the members. We sometimes met under differences of opinion, but scarcely ever failed, by conversing and reasoning, so to modify each other's ideas as to produce an unanimous result. . . .

I am not conscious that my participations in executive authority have produced any bias in favor of the single executive; because the parts I have acted have been in the subordinate, as well as superior stations, and because, if I know myself, what I have felt, and what I have wished, I know that I have never been so well pleased, as when I could shift power from my own, on the shoulders of others; nor have I ever been able to conceive how any rational being could propose happiness to himself from the exercise of power over others . . .

But the true barriers of our liberty in this country are our State governments: and the wisest conservative power ever contrived by man, is that of which our Revolution and present government found us possessed. Seventeen distinct States, amalgamated into one as to their foreign concerns, but single and independent as to their internal administration, regularly organized with a legislature and governor resting on the choice of the people, and enlightened by a free press, can never be so fascinated by the arts of one man, as to submit voluntarily to his usurpation. Nor can they be constrained to it by any force he can possess. While that may paralyze the single State in which it happens to be encamped, sixteen others, spread over a country of two thousand miles diameter, rise up on every side, ready organized for deliberation by a constitutional legislature, and for action by their governor, constitutionally the commander of the militia of the State, that is to say, of every man in it, able to bear arms; and that militia, too, regularly formed into regiments and battalions, into infantry, cavalry, and artillery, trained under officers general and subordinate, legally appointed, always in readiness, and to whom they are already in habits of obedience. The republican government of France was lost without a struggle, because the party of *un et indivisible* had prevailed:

no provincial organizations existed to which the people might rally under the authority of the laws, the seats of the directory were virtually vacant, and a small force sufficed to turn the legislature out of their chamber and to salute its leader chief of the nation. But with us, sixteen out of seventeen States rising in mass, under regular organization and legal commanders, united in object and action by their Congress, or if that be in *duress,* by a special convention, present such obstacles to an usurper as for ever to stifle ambition in the first conception of that object. . . .

Dangers of another kind might more reasonably be apprehended from this perfect and distinct organization, civil and military, of the States; to wit, that certain States, from local and occasional discontents, might attempt to secede from the Union. This is certainly possible; and would be befriended by this regular organization. But it is not probable that local discontents can spread to such an extent, as to be able to face the sound parts of so extensive an union: and if ever they could reach the majority, they would then become the regular government, acquire the ascendency in Congress, and be able to redress their own grievances by laws peaceably and constitutionally passed.[22]

Sharp and irreconcilable differences between the Federalist and Republican parties began to appear during the period when Jefferson was Secretary of State. Washington had no difficulty in moderating conflicts between Jefferson and Hamilton at his "cabinet" conferences in New York. These schisms, however, became much more serious after John Adams became president.

Division of the Parties

To William Short. Monticello, January 8, 1825.

When I arrived at New York in 1790, to take a part in the administration, being fresh from the French revolution, while in its first and pure stage, and consequently somewhat whetted up in my Republican principles, I found a state of things, in the general society of the place, which I could not have supposed possible. Being a stranger there, I was feasted from table to table, at large set dinners, the parties generally from twenty to thirty. The revolution I had left, and that we had just gone through in the decent change of our own government, being the common topics of conversation. I was astonished to find the general prevalence of monarchial sentiments, insomuch that in maintaining those of Republicanism, I had always the whole company on my hands, never scarcely finding among them a single co-advocate in that argument, unless some old member of Congress happened to be present. The furthest that any one would go, in support of the Republican features of our new government, would be to say, "The present Constitution is well as a beginning, and may be allowed a fair trial; but it is, in fact, only a stepping stone to something better." Among the writers, Denny, the editor of the *Portfolio,* who was a kind of oracle with them, and styled the Addison of America, openly avowed his preference of monarchy over all other forms of government, prided himself on the avowal, and maintained it by argument freely and without reserve, in his publications. I do not, myself, know that the Essex junto of Boston were monarchists, but I have always heard it so said and never doubted. . . . Monarchy, to be sure, is now defeated and they wish it should be forgotten that it was ever advocated. They see that it is desperate, and treat its imputation to them as a calumny; and I verily believe that none of them have it now in direct aim. Yet the spirit is not done away. The same party takes now what they deem to be next best ground, the consolidation of the government; the giving to the Federal member of the government, by unlimited constructions of the Constitution, a control over all the functions of the States, and the concentration of all power ultimately at Washington.[1]

To William Short. 1793.

There are in the United States some characters of opposite principles; some of them are high in office; others possessing great wealth, and all of them hostile to France and fondly looking to England as the staff of their hope. Their prospects have certainly not brightened. Excepting them, this country is entirely Republican, friends to the Constitution, anxious to preserve it and to have it administered according to its own Republican principles. The little party above mentioned have espoused it only as a stepping stone to monarchy and have endeavored to approximate it to that in its administration in order to render its final transition more easy. The successes of Republicanism in France have given the *coup de grace* to their prospects and I hope to their projects.[2]

To Robert Livingston. 1800.

The Constitution to which we are all attached was meant to be Republican, and we believe to be Republican according to every candid interpretation. Yet we have seen it so interpreted and administered as to be truly what the French have called a *monarchie masque*. So long has the vessel run on this way and been trimmed to it that to put her on her Republican tack will require all the skill, the firmness and the zeal of her ablest and best friends.[3]

Reply to an address of the Mayor of Alexandria. 1790.

Convinced that the Republican is the only form of government which is not eternally at open or secret war with the rights of mankind, my prayers and efforts shall be cordially distributed to the support of that we have so happily established. It is indeed an animating thought that, while we are securing the rights of ourselves and our posterity, we are pointing out the way to struggling nations who wish like us, to emerge from their tyrannies also. Heaven help their struggles and lead them, as it has done us, triumphantly through them.[4]

To George Washington. Paris, May 10, 1789.

Though we have not heard of the actual opening of the New Congress and consequently have not official information of your election as President of the U. S. yet as there never could be a doubt entertained of it, permit me to express here my felicitations, not to yourself but to my country. Nobody who has tried both public and private life can doubt but that you were much happier on the banks of the Potomac than you will be at New York. But there was nobody so well qualified as yourself to put our new machine into a regular course of action, nobody the authority of whose name could so effectually have crushed opposition at home, and produced respect abroad. I am sensible of the immensity of the sacrifice on your part. Your measure of fame was full to the brim; and therefore you have nothing to gain. But there are cases wherein it is a duty to risk all against nothing, and I believe this was exactly the case.[5]

To Harry Innes. Philadelphia, March 13, 1791.

It is fortunate that our first executive magistrate is purely and zealously Republican. We cannot expect all his successors to be so, and therefore should avail ourselves the present day to establish principles and examples which may fence us against future heresies preached now, to be practiced hereafter.[6]

To Mr. Melish. 1813.

You expected to discover the difference of our party principles in General Washington's valedictory and my inaugural address. Not at all. General Washington did not harbor one principle of Federalism. He was neither an Angloman, a monarchist, nor a separatist. He sincerely wished the people to have as much self-government as they were competent to exercise themselves. The only point on which he and I ever differed in opinion was that I had more confidence than he had in the natural integrity and discretion of the people, and in the safety and extent to which they might trust themselves with a control over their government. He has expressed to me a thousand times his determination that the existing government should have a fair trial and that in support of it, he would spend the last drop of his blood.[7]

To Thomas Law, Esq. Poplar Forest, June 13, 1814.

. . . and protest against the language of Helvetius "what other motive than self-interest could determine a man to generous actions? It is impossible for him to love what is good for the sake of good, as to love evil for the sake of evil." The Creator would indeed have been a bungling artist, had he intended man for a social animal without planting in him social dispositions. It is true they are not planted in every man, because there is no rule without exceptions; but it is false reasoning which converts exceptions into the general rule. Some men are born without the organs of sight, or of hearing, or without hands. Yet it would be wrong to say that man is born without these faculties, and sight, hearing, and hands may with truth enter into the general definition of man.

The want or imperfection of the moral sense in some men, like the want or imperfection of the senses of sight and hearing in others, is no proof that it is a general characteristic of the species. . . . I sincerely, then, believe with you in the general existence of a moral instinct. I think it the brightest gem with which the human character is studded, and the want of it as more degrading than the most hideous of the bodily deformities.[8]

To Rev. James Madison. 1795.

I am conscious that an equal division of property is impracticable. But the consequences of enormous inequality producing so much misery to the bulk of mankind, legislators cannot invent too many devices for subdividing property, only taking care to let their subdivisions go hand in hand with the natural affections of the human mind. The descent of property of every kind therefore to all the children, or to all the brothers and sisters, or other relations in equal degree is a politic measure, and a practicable one. Another means of silently lessening the inequality of property is to exempt all from taxation below a certain point and to tax the higher portions of property in geometrical progression as they rise.[9]

To Benjamin Franklin. Virginia, August 13, 1777.

With respect to the State of Virginia in particular, the people seem to have laid aside the monarchial, and taken up the republican government, with as much ease as would have attended their throwing off an old and putting on a new suit of clothes. Not a single throe has attended this important transformation. A half-dozen aristocratical gentlemen, agonizing under the loss of pre-eminence, have sometimes ventured their sarcasms on our political metamorphosis. They have been thought fitter objects of pity, than of punishment.[10]

To James Madison. Paris, March 15, 1789.

I know there are some among us who would now establish a monarchy. But they are inconsiderable in number and weight of character. The rising race are all republicans. We are educated in royalism; no wonder if some of us retain that idolatry still. Our young people are educated in republicanism; an apostasy from that to royalism is unprecedented and impossible.[11]

To Thomas Paine. Philadelphia, June 19, 1792.

Would you believe it possible that in this country there should be high and important characters who need your lessons in republicanism and do not heed them? It is but too true that we have a sect preaching up and panting after an English constitution of kings, lords, and commons, and whose heads are itching for crowns, coronets and mitres. But our people, my good friend, are firm and unanimous in their principles of republicanism, and there is no better proof of it than that they love what you write and read it with delight.[12]

From Kentucky Resolutions. *1798.*

It would be a dangerous delusion were a confidence in the men of our choice to silence our fears for the safety of our rights; confidence is everywhere the parent of despotism—free Government is founded on jealousy, and not in confidence; it is jealousy and not confidence which prescribes limited Constitutions to bind down those whom we are obliged to trust with power; our Constitution has accordingly fixed the limits to which, and no further, our confidence may go; and let the honest advocate of confidence read the Alien and Sedition acts and say if the Constitution has not been wise in fixing limits to the government it created, and whether we should be wise in destroying those limits. In questions of power, then, let no more be heard of confidence in man, but bind him down from mischief by the chains of the Constitution.[13]

From Notes on Virginia. *1792.*

Our sister States of Pennsylvania and New York have

long subsisted without any establishment at all. The experiment was new and doubtful when they made it. It has answered beyond conception. They flourish infinitely. Religion is well supported; of various kinds indeed, but all good enough; all sufficient to preserve peace and order; or if a sect arises whose tenets would subvert morals, good sense has fair play, and reason laughs it out of doors, without suffering the State to be troubled with it. Their harmony is unparalleled, and can be ascribed to nothing but their unbounded tolerance, because there is no other circumstance in which they differ from every nation on earth. They have made the happy discovery, that the way to silence religious disputes is to take no notice of them.[14]

To Francis Eppes. 1781.

You ask my opinion of Lord Bolingbroke and Thomas Paine. They were alike in making bitter enemies of the priests and Pharisees of their day. Both were honest men; both advocates for human liberty. Paine wrote for a country which prevented him to push his reasoning to whatever length it would go. Lord Bolingbroke in one restrained by a constitution, and by public opinion. He was indeed a Tory; but his writings prove him a stronger advocate for liberty than any of his countrymen, the Whigs of the present day. Irritated by his exile, he committed one act unworthy of him, in connecting himself momentarily with a prince rejected by his country. But he redeemed that single act by his establishment of the principles which proved it to be wrong. These two persons differed remarkably in the style of their writing, each leaving a model of what is most perfect in both extremes of the simple and the sublime. No writer has exceeded Paine in ease and familiarity of style, in perspicuity of expression, happiness of elucidation, and in simple and unassuming language. In this he may be compared to Dr. Franklin; and indeed his *Common Sense* was for a while believed to have been written by Dr. Franklin, and published under the borrowed name of Paine, who had come over with him from England. Lord Bolingbroke's, on the other hand, is a style of the highest order. The lofty, rhythmical, full-flowing eloquence of Cicero! Periods of just measure, their members proportioned, their close full and round. His conceptions too, are bold and strong, his doctrine copious, polished and commanding as his subject. His writings are certainly the finest samples in the English language of the eloquence proper for the Senate.[15]

To Horatio Gates. Philadelphia, February 21, 1798.

Dear General—I received duly your welcome favor of the 15th, and had an opportunity of immediately delivering the one it enclosed to General Kosciusko. I see him often, and with great pleasure mixed with commiseration. He is as pure a son of liberty as I have ever known, and of that liberty which is to go to all, and not to the few or the rich alone.[16]

To Jeremiah Moor. Monticello, August 14, 1800.

Sir—I have to acknowledge the receipt of your favor of July 12. The times are certainly such as to justify anxiety on the subject of political principles, and particularly those of the public servants. I have been so long on the public theatres that I supposed mine to be generally known.

I make no secret of them: on the contrary I wish them known to avoid the imputation of those which are not mine. You may remember perhaps that in the year 1783 after the close of the war there was a general idea that a convention would be called in this state to form a constitution. In that expectation I then prepared a scheme of constitution which I meant to have proposed. This is bound up at the end of the *Notes on Virginia,* which being in many hands, I may venture to refer to it as giving a general view of my principles of government. It particularly shows what I think on the question of the right of electing and being elected, which is principally the subject of your letter. I found it there on a year's residence in the country; or the possession of property in it, or a year's enrollment in its militia. When the constitution of Virginia was formed I was in attendance at Congress. Had I been there I should probably have proposed a general suffrage: because my opinion has always been in favor of it. Still I find very honest men who, thinking the possession of some property necessary to give due independence of mind, are for restraining the elective franchise to property. I believe we may lessen the danger of buying and selling votes, by making the number of voters too great for any means of purchase: I may further say that I have not observed men's honesty to increase with their riches.[17]

From a proposed Constitution for Virginia. 1776.

All male persons of full age and sane mind having a freehold estate (¼ of an acre) of land in any town, or in 25 acres of land in the country, and all persons resident in the colony who shall have paid scot & lot to government the last two years shall have right to give their vote in the election of their respective representatives. And every person so qualified to elect shall be capable of being elected; provided he shall have given no bribe either directly or indirectly to any elector . . .[18]

To Dupont de Nemours. 1816.

In the constitution of Spain, as proposed by the late Cortes, there was a principle entirely new to me, and not noticed in yours, that no person, born after that day, should ever acquire the rights of citizenship until he could read and write. It is impossible sufficiently to estimate the wisdom of this provision. Of all those which have been thought of for securing fidelity in the administration of the government, constant ralliance to the principles of the constitution, and progressive amendments with the progressive advances of the human mind, or changes in human affairs, it is the most effectual. Enlighten the people generally, and tyranny and oppression of body and mind will vanish like evil spirits at the dawn of day. Although I do not, with some enthusiasts, believe that the human condition will ever advance to such a state of perfection as that there shall no longer be pain or vice in the world, yet I believe it susceptible of much improvement, and most of all in matters of government and religion; and that the diffusion of knowledge among the people is to be the instrument by which it is to be effected.[19]

To James Sullivan. 1805.

If we suffer ourselves to be frightened from our post by mere lying, surely the enemy will use that weapon; for what one so cheap to those of whose system of politics morality makes no part? The patriot, like the Christian, must learn to bear revilings and persecutions as part of his duty; and in proportion as the trial is severe, firmness under it becomes more requisite and praiseworthy. It requires, indeed, self-command. But that will be fortified in proportion as the calls for its exercise are repeated.[20]

To Joseph Priestley. 1802.

In the great work which has been effected in America, no individual has a right to take any great share to himself. Our people in a body are wise, because they are under the unrestrained and unperverted operation of their own understandings. Those whom they have assigned to the direction of their affairs have stood with pretty even front. If any one of them was withdrawn many others entirely equal, have been ready to fill his place with as good abilities. A nation, composed of such materials, and free in all its members from distressing wants, furnishes hopeful implements for the interesting experiment of self-government; and we feel that we are acting under obligations not confined to the limits of our own society. It is impossible not to be sensible that we are acting for all mankind; that circumstances denied to others, but indulged to us, have imposed on us the duty of proving what is the degree of freedom and self-government in which a society may venture to have its individual members.[21]

To Mr. Leiper. 1815.

I wish that all nations may recover and retain their independence; that those which are overgrown may not advance beyond safe measures of power, that a salutary balance may be ever maintained among nations, and that our peace, commerce, and friendship may be sought and cultivated by all. It is our business to manufacture for ourselves whatever we can, to keep our markets open for what we can spare or want; and the less we have to do with the amities and enmities of Europe, the better. Not in our day, but in no distant one, we may shake a rod over the heads of all, which may make the stoutest of them tremble. But I hope our wisdom will grow with our power, and teach us, that the less we use our power, the greater it will be.[22]

To Joseph Priestley. 1800.

The Gothic idea that we are to look backwards instead of forwards for the improvement of the human mind, and to recur to the annals of our ancestors for what is not perfect in government, in religion and in learning, is worthy of those bigots in religion and government by whom it has been recommended and whose purposes it would answer. But it is not an idea which this country will endure.[23]

To H. G. Spafford. 1814.

I join in your reprobation of our merchants, priests and lawyers, for their adherence to England and monarchy, in preference to their own country and its constitutions. But merchants have no country. The mere spot they stand on does not constitute so strong an attachment as that from which they draw their gains. In every country and in every age, the priest has been hostile to liberty. He is always in alliance with the despot, abetting his abuses in return for protection to his own . . . they have perverted the best religion ever preached to man into mystery and jargon, unintelligible to all mankind, and therefore the safer engine for their purposes. With the lawyers it is a new thing. They have, in the mother country, been generally the primest supporters of the free principles of their constitution. But there, too, they have changed. I ascribe most of this to the substitution of Blackstone for my Lord Coke, as an elementary work. In truth, Blackstone and Hume have made tories of all England, and are making tories of those young Americans whose native feelings of independence do not place them above the wily sophistries of a Hume or a Blackstone.[24]

To Benjamin Austin. 1816.

We must now place the manufacturer by the side of the agriculturist. The former question is suppressed or assumes a new form. Shall we make our own comforts, or go without them, at the will of a foreign nation? He, therefore, who is against domestic manufacture, must be for reducing us either to dependence on that foreign nation, or to be clothed in skins, and to live like wild beasts in dens and caverns. I am not one of these; experience has taught me that manufactures are now as necessary to our independence as to our comfort; and if those who quote me as of a different opinion, will keep pace with me in purchasing nothing foreign where an equivalent of domestic fabric can be obtained, without regard to difference of price, it will not be our fault if we do not soon have a supply at home equal to our demand, and wrest that weapon of distress from the hand which has wielded it.[25]

To Gideon Granger. 1800.

Our country is too large to have all its affairs directed by a single government. Public service at such a distance, and from under the eye of their constituents, must, from the circumstance of distance, be unable to administer and overlook all the details necessary for the good government of the citizens and the same circumstance, by rendering detection impossible to their constituents, will invite the public agents to corruption, plunder and waste. And I do verily believe that if the principle were to prevail of a common law being in force in the United States (which principle possesses the general government at once of all the powers of the State governments) it would become the most corrupt government on the earth. . . . What an augmentation of the field, for jobbing, speculating, plundering, office-building and office-hunting would be produced by an assumption of all the State powers into the hand of the general government! The true theory of our Constitution is surely the wisest and best, that the States are independent as to everything within themselves and united as to everything respecting foreign nations. Let the general government be reduced to foreign concerns only, and let our affairs be disentangled from those of all other nations, except as to commerce, which the merchants will manage, the better the more they are left free to manage for themselves, and the general government may be reduced to a very simple organization and a very inexpensive one.[26]

To John Norvell. Washington, June 14, 1807.

Sir—Your letter of May the 9th has been duly received. The subject it proposes would require time and space for even moderate development. My occupations limit me to a very short notice of them. I think there does not exist a good elementary work on the organization of society into civil government: I mean a work which presents in one full and comprehensive view the system or principles on which such an organization should be founded, according to the rights of nature. For want of a single work of that character, I should recommend Locke on Government, Sidney, Priestley's *Essay on the First Principles of Government,* Chipman's *Principles of Government,* and the *Federalist.* Adding perhaps, Beccaria on crimes and punishments, because of the demonstrative manner in which he has treated that branch of the subject. If your views of political inquiry go further, to the subjects of money and commerce, Smith's *Wealth of Nations* is the best book to be read, unless Say's *Political Economy* can be had, which treats the same subjects on the same principles, but in a shorter compass and more lucid manner. But I believe this work has not been translated into our language.

History, in general, only informs us what bad government is. But as we have employed some of the best materials of the British constitution in the construction of our own government, a knowledge of British history becomes useful to the American politician. There is, however, no general history of that country which can be recommended. The elegant one of Hume seems intended to disguise and discredit the good principles of the government, and is so plausible and pleasing in its style and manner, as to instil its errors and heresies insensibly into the minds of unwary readers.[27]

To Mr. Thomas M. Randolph. New York, May 30, 1790.

In political economy, I think Smith's *Wealth of Nations* the best book extant; in the science of government, Montesquieu's *Spirit of Laws* is generally recommended. It contains, indeed, a great number of political truths; but also an equal number of heresies: so that the reader must be constantly on his guard. There has been lately published a letter of Helvetius, who was the intimate friend of Montesquieu, and whom he consulted before the publication of his book. Helvetius advised him not to publish it; and in this letter to a friend he gives us a solution for the mixture of truth and error found in this book. He says Montesquieu was a man of immense reading; that he had commonplaced all his reading, and that his object was to throw the whole contents of his commonplace book into systematical order, and to show his ingenuity by reconciling the contradictory facts it presents. Locke's little book on Government, is perfect as far as it goes.[28]

To Vander Kemp. 1812.

The only orthodox object of the institution of government is to secure the greatest degree of happiness possible to the general mass of those associated under it. . . . Unless the mass retains sufficient control over those intrusted with the powers of their government, these will be perverted to their own oppression, and to the perpetuation of wealth and power in the individuals and their families selected for the trust. Whether our Constitution has hit on the exact degree of control necessary, is yet under experiment; and it is a most encouraging reflection that distance and other difficulties securing us against the brigand governments of Europe, in the safe enjoyment of our farms and firesides, the experiment stands a better chance of being satisfactorily made here than on any occasion yet presented by history.[29]

To Dupont de Nemours. 1816.

But when we come to the moral principles on which the government is to be administered, we come to what is proper for all conditions of society. I meet you there in all the benevolence and rectitude of your native character; and I love myself always most where I concur most with you. Liberty, truth, probity, honor, are declared to be the four cardinal principles of your society. I believe with you that morality, compassion, generosity, are innate elements of the human constitution . . .[30]

To Monsieur D' Ivernois. Monticello, February 6, 1795.

The smaller the societies, the more violent and more convulsive their schisms. We have chanced to live in an age which will probably be distinguished in history, for its experiments in government on a larger scale than has yet taken place. But we shall not live to see the result. The grosser absurdities, such as hereditary magistracies, we shall see exploded in our day, long experience having already pronounced condemnation against them. But what is to be the substitute? This our children or grandchildren will answer. We may be satisfied with the certain knowledge that none can ever be tried, so stupid, so unrighteous, so oppressive, so destructive of every end for which honest men enter into government, as that which their forefathers had established, and their fathers alone venture to tumble headlong from the stations they have so long abused. It is unfortunate, that the efforts of mankind to recover the freedom of which they have been so long deprived, will be accompanied with violence, with errors, and even with crimes. But while we weep over the means, we must pray for the end.[32]

To John Adams. Monticello, January 11, 1816.

The idea of representative government had taken root and growth among them. Their masters feel it, and are saving themselves by timely offers of this modification of their powers. Belgium, Prussia, Poland, Lombardy, etc., are now offered a representative organization; illusive probably at first, but it will grow into power in the end. Opinion is power, and that opinion will come. Even France will yet attain representative government. You observe it makes the basis of every Constitution which has been demanded or offered,—of that demanded by their Senate; of that offered by Bonaparte; and of that granted by Louis XVIII.[33]

To Joseph C. Cabell. Monticello, February 2, 1816.

As Cato, then, concluded every speech with the words, "Carthago delenda est," so do I every opinion, with the injunction, "divide the counties into wards." Begin them only for a single purpose; they will soon show for what others they are the best instruments. God bless you, and all our rulers, and give them the wisdom, as I am sure they have the will, to fortify us against the degeneracy of our government, and the concentration of all its powers in the hands of the one, the few, the well-born or the many.[34]

To T. J. Randolph. 1808.

But in stating prudential rules for our government in society, I must not omit the important one of never entering into a dispute or argument with another. I never saw an instance of one of two disputants convincing the other by argument. I have seen many, on their getting warm, becoming rude, and shooting one another. Conviction is the effect of our own dispassionate reasoning, either in solitude, or weighing within ourselves, dispassionately, what we hear from others, standing unconvicted in argument ourselves. It was one of the rules, which, above all others, made Dr. Franklin the most amiable of men in society, "Never to contradict anybody." If he was urged to announce an opinion he did it rather by asking questions, as if for information or by suggesting doubts. When I hear another express an opinion which is not mine, I say to myself, he has a right to his opinion, as I to mine; why should I question it? His error does me no injury, and shall I become a Don Quixote to bring all men by force of argument to one opinion? If a fact be misstated, it is probable he is gratified by the belief of it, and I have no right to deprive him of the gratification. If he wants reformation he will ask it, and then I will give it in measured terms; but if he still believes his own story, and shows a desire to dispute the fact with me, I hear him and say nothing. It is his affair, not mine, if he prefers error.

There are two classes of disputants most frequently to be met among us. The first is of young students, just entered the threshold of science, with a first view of its outlines, not yet filled up with the details and modifications which a further progress would bring to their knowledge.

The other consists of the ill-tempered and rude men in society, who have taken up a passion for politics. (Good humor and politeness never introduces into a mixed society a question on which they foresee there will be a difference of opinion.) From both of these classes of disputants, my dear Jefferson, keep aloof as you would from the infected subjects of yellow fever or pestilence. Consider yourself when with them as among the patients of Bedlam, needing medical more than moral counsel. Be a listener only, keep within yourself, and endeavor to establish with yourself the habit of silence, especially in politics. In the fevered state of our country no good can ever result from any attempt to set one of these fiery zealots to rights, either in fact or principle. They are determined as to the facts they will believe and the opinions on which they will act. Get by them, therefore, as you would by an angry bull; it is not for a man of sense to dispute the road with such an animal.[35]

In 1798 the Federalists had become known as a "war party" and under their regime, private citizens were systematically harassed and spied upon, mail was illegally opened and the civil rights of many American citizens were violated by the enforcement of the Alien and Sedition Laws. Jefferson organized the Republican opposition to these measures in numerous letters and particularly in the Kentucky Resolutions, reprinted in their entirety in this chapter. Jefferson firmly believed that such violations of republican principles would be repudiated by the American people and his confidence in their good judgment was completely vindicated in two presidential elections. He was re-elected to his second term as president by a landslide vote.

Alien and Sedition Laws

To Edmund Randolph, Attorney General, May 8, 1793.

I have been still reflecting on the draught of the letter from the Secretary of the Treasury to the Custom house officers, instructing them to be on the watch as to all infractions or tendencies to infraction of the laws of neutrality by our citizens and to communicate the same to him. When this paper was first communicated to me, tho' the whole of it struck me disagreeably, I did not in the first moment see clearly the improprieties but of the last clause. The more I have reflected, the more objectionable the whole appears.

By this proposal the Collectors of the customs are to be made an established corps of spies or informers against their fellow citizens, whose actions they are to watch in secret, inform against in secret to the Secretary of the Treasury, who is to communicate it to the President. If the action and evidence appear to justify a prosecution, a prosecution is to be set on foot on the *secret information of a collector*. If it will not justify it, then the only consequence is that the mind of government has been poisoned against a citizen, neither knowing or suspecting it, and perhaps too distant to bring forward his justification. This will at least furnish the collector with a convenient weapon to keep down a rival, draw a cloud over an inconvenient censor, or satisfy mere malice and private enmity.

The object of this new institution is to be to prevent infractions of the laws of neutrality, and to preserve our peace with foreign nations. Acts involving war, or proceedings which respect foreign nations, seem to belong either to the department of war, or to that which is charged with the affairs of foreign nations. But I cannot possibly conceive how the superintendance of the laws of neutrality, or the preservation of our peace with foreign nations can be ascribed to the department of the treasury, which I suppose to comprehend merely matters of revenue. It would be to add a new and a large field to a department already amply provided with business, patronage, and influence.— It was urged as a reason, that the collectors of the customs are in convenient positions for this espionage. They are in convenient positions too for building ships of war: but will that business be transplanted from its department, merely because it can be conveniently done in another?

It seemed the desire that if this means was disapproved, some other equivalent might be adopted.—Tho' we consider the acts of a foreigner making a capture within our limits, as an act of public hostility, and therefore to be turned over to the military, rather than the civil power; yet the acts of our own citizens infringing the laws of neutrality, or contemplating that, are offenses against the ordinary laws and cognisable by them. Grand juries are the constitutional inquisitors and informers of the country, they are scattered everywhere, see everything, see it while they suppose themselves mere private persons, and not with the prejudiced eye of a permanent and systematic spy. Their information is on *oath,* is public, it is in the vicinage of the party charged, and can be at once refuted. These officers taken only occasionally from among the people, are familiar to them, the office respected, and the experience of centuries has shown that it is safely entrusted with our character, property and liberty. A grand juror cannot carry on systematic persecution against a neighbor whom he hates, because he is not permanent in the office.—The Judges generally by a charge, instruct the Grand jurors in the infractions of law which are to be noticed by them; and our Judges are in the habit of printing their charges in the newspapers. The Judges having notice of the proclamation, will perceive that the occurrence of a foreign war has brought into activity the laws of neutrality, as a part of the law of the land. This new branch of the law they will know needs explanation to the grand juries more than any other. They will study and define the subjects to them and to the public. The public mind will by this be warned against the acts which may endanger our peace, foreign nations will see a much more respectable evidence of our *bona fide* intentions to preserve neutrality, and society will be relieved from the inquietude which must forever be excited by the knowledge of the existence of such a poison in it as secret accusation. It will be easy to suggest this matter to the attention of the judges, and that alone puts the whole machine into motion. The one is a familiar, impartial and precious instrument, the other, not popular in its present functions, will be odious in the new ones, and the odium will reach the Executive who will be considered as having planted a germ of private inquisition absolutely unknown to our laws.—I am not quite certain what was considered as agreed upon yesterday, it cannot be too late however to suggest the substitution of the Judges and grand-jurors in place of the collectors of the customs.

P. S. I understood Col. H. yesterday that he should confer with the President on the subject of our deliberation. As that is not exactly the channel through which I would wish my objections to be represented, should the President mention the subject to you I will thank you to communicate to him this note, or its substance.[1]

To James Madison. Philadelphia, May 3, 1798.

Dear Sir, I wrote to you last on the 26th; since which yours of the 22nd of April has been received, acknowledging mine of the 12th; so that all appear to have been received to that date. The spirit kindled up in the towns is wonderful. These and New Jersey are pouring in their addresses, offering life and fortune. Even these addresses are not the worst things. For indiscreet declarations and expressions of passion may be pardoned to a multitude acting from the impulse of the moment. But we cannot expect a foreign nation to show that apathy to the answers of the President, which are more thrasonic than the addresses. Whatever chance for peace might have been left us after the publication of the dispatches, is completely lost by these answers. Nor is it France alone, but his own fellow-citizens, against whom his threats are uttered. In Fenno, of yesterday, you will see one, wherein he says to the address from Newark, "The delusions and misrepresentations which have misled so many citizens, must be discountenanced by authority as well as by the citizens at large"; evidently alluding to those letters from the Representatives to their constituents, which they have been in the habit of seeking after and publishing: while those sent by the tory part of the House to their constituents, are ten times more numerous, and replete with the most atrocious falsehoods and calumnies. What new law they will propose on this subject, has not yet leaked out. The citizen-bill sleeps. The alien-bill, proposed by the Senate, has not yet been brought in. That proposed by the House of Representatives has been so moderated, that it will not answer the passionate purposes of the war gentlemen. Whether, therefore, the Senate will push their bolder plan, I know not. The provisional army does not go down so smoothly in the House as it did in the Senate. They are whittling away some of its choice ingredients; particularly that of transferring their own constitutional discretion over the raising of armies to the President. A committee of the Representatives have struck out his discretion, and hang the raising of the men on the contingencies of invasion, insurrection, or declaration of war. Were all our members here, the bill would not pass. But it will, probably, as the House now is. Its expense is differently estimated, from five to eight millions of dollars a year. Their purposes before voted, require two millions above all the other taxes, which, therefore, are voted to be raised on lands, houses, and slaves. The provisional army will be additional to this. The threatening appearances from the alien-bills have so alarmed the French who are among us, that they are going off. A ship, chartered by themselves for this purpose, will sail within about a fortnight for France, with as many as she can carry. Among these I believe will be Volney, who has in truth been the principal object aimed at by the law . . .

As there is nothing material now to be proposed, we

generally expect to rise in about three weeks. However, I do not venture to order my horses.

My respectful salutations to Mrs. Madison. To yourself affectionate friendship and adieu.[2]

To James Lewis, Junior. Philadelphia, May 9, 1798.

Dear Sir, I am much obliged by your friendly letter of the 4th instant. As soon as I saw the first of Mr. Martin's letters, I turned to the newspaper of the day, and found Logan's speech, as translated by a common Indian interpreter. The version I had used, had been made by General Gibson. Finding from Mr. Martin's style, that his object was not merely truth, but to gratify party passions, I never read another of his letters. I determined to do my duty by searching into the truth, and publishing it to the world, whatever it should be. This I shall do at a proper season. I am much indebted to many persons, who, without any acquaintance with me, have voluntarily sent me information on the subject. Party passions are indeed high. Nobody has more reason to know it than myself. I receive daily bitter proofs of it from people who never saw me, nor know any thing of me but through Porcupine or Fenno. At this moment all the passions are boiling over, and one who keeps himself cool and clear of the contagion, is so far below the point of ordinary conversation, that he finds himself insulated in every society. However, the fever will not last. War, land-tax, and stamp-tax are sedatives which must cool its ardor. They will bring on reflection, and that, with information, is all which our countrymen need, to bring themselves and affairs to rights. They are essentially republicans. They retain unadulterated the principles of

'75, and those who are conscious of no change in themselves have nothing to fear in the long run. It is our duty still to endeavor to avoid war: but if it shall actually take place, no matter by whom brought on, we must defend ourselves. If our house be on fire, without inquiring whether it was fired from within or without, we must try to extinguish it. In that, I have no doubt, we shall act as one man. But if we can ward off actual war till the crisis of England is over, I shall hope we may escape it altogether.[3]

To James Madison. Philadelphia, June 7, 1798.

The Alien bill . . . is reported again very much softened, and if the proviso can be added to it, saving treaties, it will be less objectionable than I thought it possible to have obtained . . . They have have brought into the lower house a sedition bill which among other enormities, undertakes to make printing certain matters criminal, tho' one of the amendments to the Constitution has so expressly taken religion, printing presses, etc., out of their coercion. Indeed this bill and the alien bill both are so palpably in the teeth of the Constitution as to shew they mean to pay no respect to it.[4]

To Archibald Hamilton Rowan. Monticello, Sept. 26, 1798.

Sir,—To avoid the suspicions and curiosity of the post office, which would have been excited by seeing your name and mine on the back of a letter, I have delayed acknowledging the receipt of your favor of July last, till an occasion to write to an inhabitant of Wilmington gives me an opportunity of putting my letter under cover to him. The system of alarm & jealousy which has been so powerfully played off in England, has been mimicked here, not entirely without success. The most long-sighted politician could not, seven years ago, have imagined that the people of this wide-extended country could have been enveloped in such delusion, and made so much afraid of themselves and their own power, as to surrender it spontaneously to those who are manoeuvering them into a form of government, the principal branches of which may be beyond their control. The commerce of England, however, has spread its roots over the whole face of our country. This is a real source of all the obliquities of the public mind; and I should have had doubts of the ultimate term they might attain; but happily, the game, to be worth the playing of those engaged in it, must flush them with money. The authorized expenses of this year are beyond those of any year in the late war for independence, and they are of a nature to beget great and constant expenses. The purse of the people is the real seat of sensibility. It is to be drawn upon largely, and they will then listen to truths which could not excite them through any other organ. In this State, however, the delusion has not prevailed. They are sufficiently on their guard to have justified the assurance, that should you choose it for your asylum, the laws of the land, administered by upright judges, would protect you from any exercise of power unauthorized by the Constitution of the United States. The Habeas corpus secures every man here, alien or citizen, against everything which is not law, whatever shape it may assume.[5]

To Stephens Thompson Mason. Monticello, Oct. 11, 1798.

For my own part I consider those laws as merely an experiment on the American mind, to see how far it will bear an avowed violation of the constitution. If this goes down we shall immediately see attempted another act of Congress declaring that the President shall continue in office during life, reserving to another occasion the transfer of the succession to his heirs, and the establishment of the Senate for life . . . That these things are in contemplation, I have no doubt; nor can I be confident of their failure, after the dupery of which our countrymen have shewn themselves susceptible.[6]

Kentucky Resolutions of 1798 (November)

1. *Resolved,* That the several States composing the United States of America, are not united on the principle of unlimited submission to their general government; but that, by a compact under the style and title of a Constitution for the United States, and of amendments thereto, they constituted a general government for special purposes, —delegated to that government certain definite powers, reserving, each State to itself, the residuary mass of right to their own self-government; and that whensoever the general government assumes undelegated powers, its acts are unauthoritative, void, and of no force: that to this compact each State acceded as a State, and is an integral party, its co-States forming, as to itself, the other party: that the government created by this compact was not made the exclusive or final judge of the extent of the powers delegated to itself; since that would have made its discretion, and not the Constitution, the measure of its powers; but

that, as in all other cases of compact among powers having no common judge, each party has an equal right to judge for itself, as well of infractions as of the mode and measure of redress.

2. *Resolved,* That the Constitution of the United States having delegated to Congress a power to punish treason, counterfeiting the securities and current coin of the United States, piracies, and felonies committed on the high seas, and offenses against the law of nations, and no other crimes whatsoever; and it being true as a general principle, and one of the amendments to the Constitution having also declared, that "the powers not delegated to the United States by the Constitution, nor prohibited by it to the States, are reserved to the States respectively, or to the people," therefore the act of Congress, passed on the 14th day of July, 1798, and entitled "An Act in addition to the act entitled An Act for the punishment of certain crimes against the United States," as also the act passed by them on the — day of June, 1798, entitled "An Act to punish frauds committed on the bank of the United States," (and all their other acts which assume to create, define, or punish crimes, other than those so enumerated in the Constitution,) are altogether void, and of no force; and that the power to create, define, and punish such other crimes is reserved, and, of right, appertains solely and exclusively to the respective States, each within its own territory.

3. *Resolved,* That it is true as a general principle, and is also expressly declared by one of the amendments to the Constitution, that "the powers not delegated to the United States by the Constitution, nor prohibited by it to the

States, are reserved to the States respectively, or to the people"; and that no power over the freedom of religion, freedom of speech, or freedom of the press being delegated to the United States by the Constitution, nor prohibited by it to the States, all lawful powers respecting the same did of right remain, and were reserved to the States or the people: that thus was manifested their determination to retain to themselves the right of judging how far the licentiousness of speech and of press may be abridged without lessening their useful freedom, and how far those abuses which cannot be separated from their use should be tolerated, rather than the use be destroyed. And thus also they guarded against all abridgment by the United States of the freedom of religious opinions and exercises, and retained to themselves the right of protecting the same, as this State, by a law passed on the general demand of its citizens, had already protected them from all human restraint or interference. And that in addition to this general principal and express declaration, another and more special provision has been made by one of the amendments to the Constitution, which expressly declares, that "Congress shall make no law respecting an establishment of religion, or prohibiting the free exercise thereof, or abridging the freedom of speech or of the press": thereby guarding in the same sentence, and under the same words, the freedom of religion, of speech, and of the press: insomuch, that whatever violates either, throws down the sanctuary which covers the others, and that libels, falsehood, and defamation, equally with heresy and false religion, are withheld from the cognizance of federal tribunals. That, therefore, the act of Congress of the United States, passed on the 14th day of

July, 1798, entitled "An Act in addition to the act entitled An Act for the punishment of certain crimes against the United States," which does abridge the freedom of the press is not law, but is altogether void, and of no force.

4. *Resolved,* That alien friends are under the jurisdiction and protection of the laws of the State wherein they are: that no power over them has been delegated to the United States, nor prohibited to the individual States, distinct from their power over citizens. And it being true as a general principle, and one of the amendments to the Constitution having also declared, that "the powers not delegated to the United States by the Constitution, nor prohibited by it to the States, are reserved to the States respectively, or to the people," the act of the Congress of the United States, passed on the — day of July, 1798, entitled "An Act concerning aliens," which assumes powers over alien friends, not delegated by the Constitution, is not law, but is altogether void, and of no force.

5. *Resolved,* That in addition to the general principle, as well as the express declaration, that powers not delegated are reserved, another and more special provision, inserted in the Constitution from abundant caution, has declared that "the migration or importation of such persons as any of the States now existing Shall think proper to admit, shall not be prohibited by the Congress prior to the year 1808": that this commonwealth does admit the migration of alien friends, described as the subject of the said act concerning aliens: that a provision against prohibiting their migration, is a provision against all acts equivalent thereto, or it would be nugatory: that to remove

them when migrated, is equivalent to a prohibition of their migration, and is therefore, contrary to the said provision of the Constitution, and void.

6. *Resolved,* That the imprisonment of a person under the protection of the laws of this commonwealth, on his failure to obey the simple *order* of the President to depart out of the United States, as is undertaken by said act entitled "An Act concerning aliens," is contrary to the Constitution, one amendment to which has provided that "no person shall be deprived of liberty without due process of law"; and that another having provided that "in all criminal prosecutions the accused shall enjoy the right to public trial by an impartial jury, to be informed of the nature and cause of the accusation, to be confronted with the witnesses against him, to have compulsory process for obtaining witnesses in his favor, and to have the assistance of counsel for his defense," the same act, undertaking to authorize the President to remove a person out of the United States, who is under the protection of the law, on his own suspicion, without accusation, without jury, without public trial, without confrontation of the witnesses against him, without hearing witnesses in his favor, without defense, without counsel, is contrary to the provision also of the Constitution, is therefore not law, but utterly void, and of no force: that transferring the power of judging any person, who is under the protection of the laws, from the courts to the President of the United States, as is undertaken by the same act concerning aliens, is against the article of the Constitution which provides that "the judicial power of the United States shall be vested in courts, the judges of which shall hold their offices during good behavior"; and

that the said act is void for that reason also. And it is further to be noted, that this transfer of judiciary power is to that magistrate of the general government who already possesses all the Executive, and a negative on all Legislative powers.

7. *Resolved,* That the construction applied by the General Government (as is evidenced by sundry of their proceedings) to those parts of the Constitution of the United States which delegate to Congress a power "to lay and collect taxes, duties, imposts, and excises, to pay debts, and provide for the common defense and general welfare of the United States," and "to make all laws which shall be necessary and proper for carrying into execution the powers vested by the Constitution in the government of the United States, or in any department or officer thereof," goes to the destruction of all limits prescribed to their power by the Constitution: that words meant by the instrument to be subsidiary only to the execution of limited powers, ought not to be so construed as themselves to give unlimited powers, nor a part to be so taken as to destroy the whole residue of that instrument: that the proceedings of the General Government under color of these articles, will be a fit and necessary subject of revisal and correction, at a time of greater tranquility, while those specified in the preceding resolutions call for immediate redress.

8. *Resolved,* That a committee of conference and correspondence be appointed, who shall have in charge to communicate the preceding resolutions to the Legislatures of the several States; to assure them that this commonwealth

continues in the same esteem of their friendship and union which it has manifested from that moment at which a common danger first suggested a common union: that it considers union, for specified national purposes, and particularly to those specified in the late federal compact, to be friendly to the peace, happiness, and prosperity of all the States: that faithful to that compact, according to the plain intent and meaning in which it was understood and acceded to by the several parties, it is sincerely anxious for its preservation: that it does also believe, that to take from the States all the powers of self-government and transfer them to a general and consolidated government, without regard to the special delegations and reservation solemnly agreed to in that compact, is not for the peace, happiness, or prosperity of these States; and that therefore this commonwealth is determined, as it doubts not its co-States are, to submit to undelegated, and consequently unlimited powers in no man, or body of men on earth: that in cases of an abuse of the delegated powers, the members of the general government, being chosen by the people, a change by the people would be the constitutional remedy; but, where powers are assumed which have not been delegated, a nullification of the act is the rightful remedy: that every State has a natural right in cases not within the compact, *(casus non foederis,)* to nullify of their own authority all assumptions of power by others within their limits: that without this right they would be under the dominion, absolute and unlimited, of whosoever might exercise this right of judgment for them: that nevertheless, this common wealth, from motives of regard and respect for its co-States, has wished to communicate with them on the subject: that with them alone it is proper to communicate, they alone being parties to the compact, and solely authorized to judge in the last resort of the powers exercised under it, Congress being not a party, but merely the creature of the compact, and subject as to its assumptions of power to the final judgment of those by whom, and for whose use itself and its powers were all created and modified: that if the acts before specified should stand, these conclusions would flow from them; that the general government may place any act they think proper on the list of crimes, and punish it themselves whether enumerated or not enumerated by the constitution as cognizable by them: that they may transfer its cognizance to the President, or any other person, who may himself be the accuser, counsel, judge and jury, whose *suspicions* may be the evidence, his *order* the sentence, his *officer* the executioner, and his breast the sole record of the transaction: that a very numerous and valuable description of the inhabitants of these States being, by this precedent, reduced, as outlaws, to the absolute dominion of one man, and the barrier of the Constitution thus swept away from us all, no rampart now remains against the passions and the powers of a majority in Congress to protect from a like exportation, or other more grievous punishment the minority of the same body, the legislatures, judges, governors and counsellors of the States, nor their other peaceable inhabitants, who may venture to reclaim the constitutional rights and liberties of the States and people, or who for other causes, good or bad, may be obnoxious to the views, or marked by the suspicions of the President, or be thought dangerous to his or their election, or other interests public or personal: that the friendless alien has indeed been selected as the safest subject of a first experiment; but the citizen will soon follow, or rather, has already followed, for already has a sedition act marked him as its prey: that these and successive acts of the same character, unless arrested at the threshold, necessarily drive these States into revolution and blood, and will furnish new calumnies against republican government, and new pretexts for those who wish it to be believed that man cannot be governed but by a rod of iron: that it would be a dangerous delusion were a confidence in the men of our choice to silence our fears for the safety of our rights: that confidence is everywhere the parent of despotism — free government is founded in jealousy, and not in confidence; it is jealousy and not confidence which prescribes limited constitutions, to bind down those whom we are obliged to trust with power: that our Constitution has accordingly fixed those limits to which, and no further, our confidence may go; and let the honest advocate of confidence read the Alien and Sedition acts, and say if the Constitution has not been wise in fixing limits to the government it created, and whether we should be wise in destroying those limits. Let him say what the government is, if it be not tyranny, which the men of our choice have conferred on our President, and the President of our choice has assented to, and accepted over the friendly strangers to whom the mild spirit of our country and its laws have pledged hospitality and protection: that the men of our choice have more respected the bare *suspicions* of the President, than the solid right of innocence, the claims of justification, the sacred force of truth and the forms and substance of law and justice. In questions of power, then, let no more be heard of confidence in man, but bind him down from mischief by the chains of the Constitution. That this commonwealth does therefore call on its co-States for an expression of their sentiments on the acts concerning aliens, and for the punishment of certain crimes herein before specified, plainly declaring whether these acts are or are not authorized by the federal compact. And it doubts not that their sense will be so announced as to prove their attachment unaltered to limited government, whether general or particular. And that the rights and liberties of their co-States will be exposed to no dangers by remaining embarked in a common bottom with their own. That they will concur with this commonwealth in considering the said acts as so palpably against the Constitution as to amount to an undisguised declaration that the compact is not meant to be the measure of the powers of the General Government, but that it will proceed in the exercise over these States, of all powers whatsoever: that they will view this as seizing the rights of the States, and consolidating them in the hands of the General Government, with a power assumed to bind the States, (not merely in the cases made federal, *casus foederis,* but) in all cases whatsoever, by laws made, not with their consent, but by others against their consent; that this would be to surrender the form of government we have chosen, and live under, one deriving its powers from its own will, and not from our authority; and that the co-States, recurring to their natural right in cases not made federal, will concur in declaring these acts void, and of no force, and will each take measures of its own for providing that neither these acts, nor any others of the General Government not plainly and intentionally authorized by the Constitution, shall be exercised within their respective territories.

9. *Resolved,* That the said committee be authorized to communicate by writing or personal conferences, at any times or places whatever, with any person or persons who may be appointed by any one or more co-States to correspond or confer with them; and that they lay their proceedings before the next session of Assembly.[7]

To M. N. G. Dufief. Monticello, April 19, 1814.

I am really mortified to be told that, *in the United States of America,* a fact like this can become a subject of inquiry, and of criminal inquiry too, as an offense against religion; that a question about the sale of a book can be carried before the civil magistrate. Is this then our freedom of religion? And are we to have a censor whose imprimatur shall say what books may be sold, and what we may buy? And who is thus to dogmatize religious opinions for our citizens? Whose foot is to be the measure to which ours are to be cut or stretched? Is a priest to be our inquisitor, or shall a layman, simple as ourselves, set up his reason as the rule for what we are to read and what we must believe? It is an insult to our citizens to question whether they are rational beings or not, and blasphemy against religion to suppose it cannot stand the test of truth and reason. If M. de Becourt's book be false in its facts, disprove them; if false in its reasoning refute it. But, for God's sake, let us freely hear both sides, if we choose. I know little of its contents, having barely glanced over here and there a passage, and over the table of contents. From this, the Newtonian philosophy seemed the chief object, the issue of which might be trusted to the strength of the two combatants; Newton certainly not needing the auxiliary arm of the government, and still less the holy Author of our religion, as to what in it concerns Him. I thought the work would be very innocent, and one which might be confided to the reason of any man; not likely to be much read if let alone, but, if persecuted, it will be generally read. Every man in the United States will think it a duty to buy a copy, in vindication of his right to buy, and to read what he pleases.[8]

To Gideon Granger. Monticello, March 9, 1814.

With respect to the dismission of the prosecutions for sedition in Connecticut, it is well known to have been a tenet of the republican portion of our fellow citizens, that the sedition law was contrary to the constitution and therefore void. On this ground I considered it as a nullity wherever I met it in the course of my duties; and on this ground I directed a *nolle prosequis* in all the prosecutions which had been instituted under it, and as far as the public sentiment can be inferred from the occurrences of the day, we may say that this opinion had the sanction of the nation. The prosecutions, therefore, which were afterwards instituted in Connecticut, of which two were against printers, two against preachers, and one against a judge, were too inconsistent with this principle to be permitted to go on. We were bound to administer to others the same measure of the law, not which they had meted to us, but we to ourselves, and to extend to all equally the protection of the same constitutional principles. These prosecutions, too, were chiefly for charges against myself, and I had from the beginning laid it down as a rule to notice nothing of the kind. I believed that the long course of services in which I had acted on the public stage, and under the eye of my fellow citizens, furnished better evidence to them of my character and principles, than the angry invectives of adverse partisans in whose eyes the very acts most approved by the majority were subjects of the greatest demerit and censure. These prosecutions against them, therefore, were to be dismissed as a matter of duty. But I wished it to be done with all possible respect to the worthy citizens who had advised them, and in such a way as to spare their feelings which had been justly irritated by the intemperance of their adversaries. As you were of that State and intimate with these characters, the business was confided to you, and you executed it to my perfect satisfaction.[9]

To John Cabel Breckenridge. Monticello, Dec. 11, 1821.

Dear Sir—Your letter places me under a dilemma which I cannot solve but by an exposition of the naked truth. I would have wished this rather to have remained as hitherto, without inquiry, but your inquiries have a right to be answered. I will do it as exactly as the great lapse of time and a waning of memory will enable me. I may misremember indifferent circumstances, but can be right in substance. At the time when the Republicans of our country were so much alarmed at the proceedings of the Federal ascendancy in Congress, in the Executive and the Judiciary departments, it became a matter of serious consideration how head could be made against their enterprises on the Constitution. The leading republicans in Congress found themselves of no use there, browbeaten as they were by a bold and over-whelming majority. They concluded to retire from that field, take a stand in their state legislatures, and endeavor there to arrest their progress. The Alien and Sedition laws furnished the particular occasion. The sympathy between Virginia and Kentucky was more cordial and more intimately confidential than between any other two States of republican policy. Mr. Madison came into the Virginia legislature. I was then in the Vice-Presidency, and could not leave my station; but your father, Colonel W. C. Nicholas, and myself, happening to be together, the engaging the co-operation of Kentucky in an energetic protestation against the constitutionality of those laws became a subject of consultation. Those gentlemen pressed me strongly to sketch resolutions for that purpose, your father undertaking to introduce them to that legislature, with a solemn assurance, which I strictly required, that it should not be known from what quarter they came. I drew and delivered them to him, and in keeping their origin secret he fulfilled his pledge of honor. Some years after this, Colonel Nicholas asked me if I had any objection to it being known that I had drawn them. I pointedly enjoined that it should not. Whether he had unguardedly intimated before to any one I know not, but I afterwards observed in the papers repeated imputations of them to me, on which as has been my practice on all occasions of imputation, I have observed entire silence. The question, indeed, has never before been put to me, nor should I answer it to any other than yourself, seeing no good end to be proposed by it, and the desire of tranquility inducing with me a wish to be withdrawn from public notice. Your father's zeal and talents were too well known to desire any additional distinction from the penning these resolutions. That circumstance surely was of far less merit than the proposing and carrying them through the legislature of his state. The only fact in this statement on which my memory is not distinct, is the time and occasion of the consultation with your father and Mr. Nicholas. It took place here I know, but whether any other person was present or communicated with is my doubt. I think Mr. Madison was either with us or consulted, but my memory is uncertain as to minor details. I fear, dear sir, we are now in such another crisis, with this difference only, that the judiciary branch is alone and singlehanded in the present assaults on the Constitution; but its assaults are more sure and deadly, as from an agent seemingly passive and unassuming. May you and your contemporaries meet them with the same determination and effect as your father and his did the "alien and sedition" laws and preserve inviolate a constitution which, cherished in all its chastity and purity, will prove in the end a blessing to all the nations of the earth. With these prayers, accept those for your own happiness and prosperity.[10]

Letters written during the first years of Jefferson's presidency provide an interesting commentary on this period of reconciliation. His attitude toward the press, however, was not conciliatory and appears to have gone through very little change over a long period of years.

Letters from the President

To James Monroe. Washington, February 15, 1801.

Dear Sir—I have received several letters from you which have not been acknowledged. By the post I dare not, and one or two confidential opportunities have passed me by surprise. I have regretted it the less, because I know you could be more safely and fully informed by others. Mr. Tyler, the bearer of this, will give you a great deal more information personally than can be done by letter. Four days of balloting have produced not a single change of a vote. Yet it is confidently believed by most that tomorrow there is to be a coalition. I know of no foundation for this belief. However, as Mr. Tyler waits the event of it, he will communicate it to you. If they could have been permitted to pass a law for putting the government into the hands of an officer, they would certainly have prevented an election. . . . Many attempts have been made to obtain terms and promises from me. I have declared to them unequivocally, that I would not receive the government on capitulation, that I would not go into it with my hands tied. Should they yield the election, I have reason to expect in the outset the greatest difficulties as to nominations. The late incumbents running away from their offices and leaving them vacant, will prevent my filling them without the *previous* advice of Senate. How this difficulty is to be got

109

over I know not. Accept for Mrs. Monroe and yourself my affectionate salutations. Adieu.[1]

To John Dickinson. Washington, March 6, 1801

Dear Sir—No pleasure can exceed that which I received from reading your letter of the 21st ultimo. It was like the joy we expect in the mansions of the blessed, when received with the embraces of our forefathers, we shall be welcomed with their blessing as having done our part not unworthily of them. The storm through which we have passed, has been tremendous indeed. The tough sides of our Argosie have been thoroughly tried. Her strength has stood the waves into which she was steered, with a view to sink her. We shall put her on her republican tack, and she will now show by the beauty of her motion the skill of her builders. Figure apart, our fellow-citizens have been led hood-winked from their principles by a most extraordinary combination of circumstances. But the band is removed, and they now see for themselves. I hope to see shortly a perfect consolidation, to effect which, nothing shall be spared on my part, short of the abandonment of the principles of our revolution. A just and solid republican government maintained here, will be a standing monument and example for the aim and imitation of the people of other countries; and I join with you in the hope and belief that they will see, from our example, that a free government is of all others the most energetic; that the inquiry which has been excited among the mass of mankind by our revolution and its consequences, will ameliorate the condition of man over a great portion of the globe. What a satisfaction have we in the contemplation of the benevolent effects of our efforts, compared with those of the leaders on the other side, who have discountenanced all advances in science as dangerous innovations, have endeavored to render philosophy and republicanism terms of reproach, to persuade us that man cannot be governed but by the rod, etc. I shall have the happiness of living and dying in the contrary hope. Accept assurances of my constant and sincere respect and attachment, and my affectionate salutations.[2]

To William Findley. Washington, March 24, 1801.

It will always be interesting to me to know the impression made by any particular thing on the public mind. My idea is that where two measures are equally right, it is a duty to the people to adopt that one which is most agreeable to them; and where a measure not agreeable to them has been adopted, it is desirable to know it, because it is an admonition to a review of that measure to see if it has been really right, and to correct it if mistaken. It is rare that the public sentiment decides immorally or unwisely, and the individual who differs from it ought to distrust and examine well his own opinion. As to the character of the appointments which have been, and will be made, I have less fear as to the satisfaction they will give, provided the real appointments only be attended to, and not the lying ones of which the papers are daily full. The paper which probably will be correct in that article will be Smith's, who is at hand to get his information from the offices. But as to removals from office, great differences of opinion exist. That some ought to be removed all will agree. That all should, nobody will say: And no two will probably draw the same line between these two extremes; consequently nothing like general approbation can be expected. Malconduct is a just ground of removal: mere difference of political opinion is not. The temper of some states requires a stronger procedure, that of others would be more alienated even by a milder course. Taking into consideration all circumstances we can only do in every case what to us seems best, and trust to the indulgence of our fellow-citizens who may see the same matter in a different point of view. The nominations crowded in by Mr. Adams after he knew he was not appointing for himself, I treat as mere nullities. His best friends do not disapprove of this. Time, prudence and patience will perhaps get us over this whole difficulty.[3]

To Levi Lincoln. March 24, 1802.

I had no conception there were persons enough to support a paper whose stomachs could bear such aliment as the enclosed papers contain. They are far beyond even the *Washington Federalist*. To punish however is impracticable until the body of the people, from whom injuries are to be taken, get their minds to rights; and even then I doubt its expediency. While a full range is proper for actions by individuals, either private or public, for slanders affecting them, I would wish much to see the experiment tried of getting along without public prosecutions for *libels*. I believe we can do it. Patience and well doing, instead of punishment, if it can be found sufficiently efficacious, would be a happy change in the instruments of government.[4]

To James Madison. Paris, 1788.

With respect to the *Federalist*, the three authors had been named to me. I read it with care, pleasure and improvement, and was satisfied there was nothing in it by one of these hands and not a great deal by a second. It does the highest honor to the third, as being in my opinion, the best commentary on the principles of government which ever was written. In some parts it is discoverable that the author means only to say what may best be said in defense of opinions in which he did not concur. But in general it establishes firmly the plan of government. I confess it has rectified me in several points.[5]

Anas. 1793.

His paper (Freneau) has saved our Constitution, which was galloping fast into monarchy and has been checked by no one means so powerfully as by that paper. It is well and universally known that it has been that paper which has checked the career of the Monocrats, and the President not sensible of the designs of the party has not with his usual good sense and *sang froid* looked on the efforts and effects of this free press, and seen that though some bad things have passed through it to the public yet the good have preponderated immensely.[6]

To James Monroe. May 26, 1800.

As to the calumny of Atheism, I am so broken to calumnies of every kind, from every department of government, Executive, Legislative, and Judiciary, and from every minion of theirs holding office or seeking it, that I entirely disregard it. . . . It has been so impossible to contradict all their lies, that I am determined to contradict none; for while I should be engaged with one, they would publish twenty new ones.[7]

To John Norvell. Washington, June 14, 1807.

To your request of my opinion of the manner in which a newspaper should be conducted, so as to be most useful, I should answer, "by restraining it to true facts and sound principles only." Yet I fear such a paper would find few subscribers. It is a melancholy truth, that a suppression of the press could not more completely deprive the nation of its benefits, than is done by its abandoned prostitution to falsehood. Nothing can now be believed which is seen in a newspaper. Truth itself becomes suspicious by being put into that polluted vehicle. The real extent of this state of misinformation is known only to those who are in situations to confront facts within their knowledge with the lies of the day. I really look with commiseration over the great body of my fellow citizens who, reading newspapers, live and die in the belief that they have known something of what has been passing in the world in their time; whereas, the accounts they have read in newspapers are just as true a history of any other period of the world as of the present, except that the real names of the day are affixed to their fables. General facts may indeed be collected from them, such as that Europe is now at war, that Bonaparte has been a successful warrior, that he has subjected a great portion of Europe to his will, etc., etc.; but no details can be relied upon. I will add, that the man who never looks into a newspaper is better informed than he who reads them; inasmuch as he who knows nothing is nearer to truth than he whose mind is filled with falsehoods and errors.[8]

To Thomas McKean. Washington, January 17, 1804.

Dear Sir—I have duly received your favor of the 8th but the act of ratification which it announces is not yet come to hand. No doubt it is on its way. That great opposition is and will be made by federalists to this amendment is certain. They know that if it prevails, neither a President or Vice President can ever be made but by the fair vote of the majority of the nation, of which they are not. That either their opposition to the principle of discrimination now, or their advocation of it formerly was on party, not moral motives, they cannot deny. Consequently they fix for themselves the place in the scale of moral rectitude to which they are entitled. I am a friend to the discriminating principle; and for a reason more than others have, inasmuch as the discriminated vote of my constituents will express unequivocally the verdict they wish to cast on my conduct. The abominable slanders of my political enemies have obliged me to call for that verdict from my country in the only way it can be obtained, and if obtained it will be my sufficient voucher to the rest of the world and to posterity, and leave me free to seek, at a definite time, the repose I sincerely wished to have retired to now. I suffer myself to make no inquiries as to the persons who are to be placed on the roles of competition for the public favor. Respect for myself as well as for the public requires that I should be the silent and passive subject of their consideration.[9]

To Joseph Scott. Washington, March 9, 1804.

Sir—I have duly received your favor of the 5th inst, and I hasten to assure you that neither Doctor Leib nor Mr. Duane have ever given the least hint to me that yourself or your associates of the St. Patrick's society meditated joining a third party; or schismatizing in any way from the great body of republicans. That the rudiments of such a 3rd party were formed in Pennsylvania and New York has been said in the newspapers, but not proved. Altho' I shall learn it with concern whenever it does happen, and think it possibly may happen that we shall divide among ourselves whenever federalism is completely eradicated, yet I think it the duty of every republican to make great sacrifices of opinion to put off the evil day, and that yourself and associates have as much disposition to do this as any portion of our body I have never seen reason to doubt. Recommending therefore sincerely a mutual indulgence, and candor among brethren and that we be content to obtain the best measures we can get, if we cannot get all we would wish, I tender you my salutations and respects.[10]

In a code letter written to Messrs. Carmichael and Short on March 23, 1793—a copy of this document was approved and signed by President Washington—Jefferson stresses the importance of keeping a free hand in any negotiations with France in respect to Louisiana. Just ten years later the Louisiana Territory was purchased from France in one of the most important single acts of government in our history. The long course of this negotiation, its conclusion and results, are narrated in the following letters.

Mississippi & Louisiana Territories

Observations on the Article Etats-Unis for the Encyclopedie. June 22, 1786.

The territories of the United States contain about a million of square miles, English. There is in them a greater proportion of fertile lands than in the British dominions in Europe. Suppose the territory of the U. S. then to attain an equal degree of population with the British European dominions, they will have an hundred millions of inhabitants . . . The present population of the inhabited parts of the U. S. is of about 10 to the square mile; and experience has shown us, that wherever we reach that the inhabitants become uneasy, as too much compressed, and go off in great numbers to search for vacant country. Within 40 years the whole territory will be peopled at that rate. We may fix that then as the term beyond which the people of those states will not be restrained within their present limits; we may fix it too as the term of population, which they will not exceed till the whole of those two continents are filled up to that mark, that is to say, till they shall contain 120 millions of inhabitants. The soil of the country on the Western side of the Mississippi, its climate, and its vicinity to the U. S. point it out as the first which will receive population from that nest. The present occupiers will just have force enough to repress and restrain the emigrations to a certain degree of consistence. We have seen lately a single person go and decide on a settlement in Kentucky, many hundred miles from any white inhabitant, remove thither with his family and a few neighbors, and though perpetually harassed by the Indians, that settlement in the course of 10 years has acquired 30,000 inhabitants, its numbers are increasing while we are writing, and the state of which it formerly made a part has offered it independence.[1]

To James Madison. Paris, January 30, 1787.

If these transactions give me no uneasiness, I feel very differently at another piece of intelligence, to wit, the possibility that the navigation of the Mississippi may be abandoned to Spain. I never had any interest Westward of the Alleghaney; & I never will have any. But I have had great opportunities of knowing the character of the people who inhabit that country. And I will venture to say that the act which abandons the navigation of the Mississippi is an act of separation between the Eastern & Western country. It is a relinquishment of five parts out of eight of the territory of the United States, an abandonment of the fairest subject for the payment of our public debts, & the chaining of those debts on our necks *in perpetuum.* I have the utmost confidence in the honest intentions of those who concur in this measure; but I lament their want of acquaintance with the character & physical advantages of the people who, right or wrong, will suppose their interests sacrificed on this occasion to the contrary interests of that part of the confederacy in possession of present power. If they declare themselves a separate people, we are incapable of a single effort to retain them. Our citizens can never be induced, either as militia or as soldiers, to go there to cut the throats of their brothers & sons, or rather to be themselves the subjects instead of the perpetrators of the parricide. Nor would that country requite the cost of being retained against the will of its inhabitants, could it be done. But it cannot be done. They are able already to rescue the navigation of the Mississippi out of the hands of Spain, & to add New Orleans to their own territory. They will be joined by the inhabitants of Louisiana. This will bring on a war between them & Spain; and that will produce the question with us whether it will not be worth our while to become parties with them in the war, in order to reunite them with us, & thus correct our error?[2]

To John Brown. Paris, May 26, 1788.

Dear Sir—It was with great pleasure I saw your name on the roll of Delegates, but I did not know you had actually come on to New York, till Mr. Paradise informed me of it. Your removal from Carolina to Kentucky was not an indifferent event to me. I wish to see that country in the hands of people well disposed, who know the value of the connection between that and the maritime States, and who wish to cultivate it. I consider their happiness as bound up together, and that every measure should be taken, which may draw the bands of union tighter. It will be an efficacious one to receive them into Congress, as I perceive they are about to desire. If to this be added an honest and disinterested conduct in Congress, as to every thing relating to them, we may hope for a perfect harmony. The navigation of the Mississippi was, perhaps, the strongest trial to which the justice of the federal government could be put. If ever they thought wrong about it, I trust they have got to rights. I should think it proper for the western country to defer pushing their right to that navigation to extremity, as long as they can do without it, tolerably; but that the moment it becomes absolutely necessary for them, it will become the duty of the maritime states to push it to every extremity, to which they would their own right of navigating the Chesapeake, the Delaware, the Hudson, or any other water. A time of peace will not be the surest for obtaining this object. Those, therefore, who have influence in the new country, would act wisely, to endeavor to keep things quiet till the western parts of Europe shall be engaged in war.[3]

To Mr. Carmichael. August 22, 1790.

We have a *right* to the navigation of the Mississippi— 1, by Nature; 2, by Treaty. It is *necessary* to us. More than half the territory of the United States is on the waters of that river. Two hundred thousand of our citizens are settled on them, of whom forty thousand bear arms. These have no outlet for their tobacco, rice, corn, hemp, lumber, house timber, ship timber.[4]

To Messrs. Carmichael and Short.

Philadelphia, March 23, 1793.

Gentlemen—It is intimated to us in such a way as to attract our attention, that France means to send a strong force early this spring to offer independence to the Spanish American colonies, beginning with those on the Mississippi; and that she will not object to the receiving those on the east side into our confederation. Interesting considerations require, that we should keep ourselves free to act in this case according to circumstances, and consequently, that you should not, by any clause of treaty, bind us to guaranty any of the Spanish colonies against their own independence, nor indeed against any other nation. For when we thought we might guaranty Louisiana, on their ceding the Floridas to us, we apprehended it would be seized by Great Britain, who would thus completely encircle us with her colonies and fleets. This danger is now removed by the concert between Great Britain and Spain; and the times will soon enough give independence, and consequently free commerce to our neighbors, without our risking the involving ourselves in a war for them.

I am, with great respect and esteem, your most obedient, humble servant,

TH: JEFFERSON
The above meets the approbation of
GEORGE WASHINGTON[5]*

To Robert R. Livingston, Minister to France.
Washington, April 18, 1802.

The cession of Louisiana and the Floridas by Spain to France works most sorely on the U. S. On this subject the Secretary of State has written to you fully. Yet I cannot forbear recurring to it personally, so deep is the impression it makes in my mind. It completely reverses all the political relations of the U. S. and will form a new epoch in

* This is in the handwriting of General Washington. This letter was in cipher, but a literal copy of it preserved.

our political course. Of all nations of any consideration France is the one which hitherto has offered the fewest points on which we could have any conflict of right, and the most points of a communion of interests. From these causes we have ever looked to her as our *natural friend,* as one with which we never could have an occasion of difference. Her growth therefore we viewed as our own, her misfortunes ours. There is on the globe one single spot, the possessor of which is our natural and habitual enemy. It is New Orleans, through which the produce of three-eighths of our territory must pass to market, and from its fertility it will ere long yield more than half of our whole produce and contain more than half our inhabitants. France placing herself in that door assumes to us the attitude of defiance. Spain might have retained it quietly for years. Her pacific dispositions, her feeble state, would induce her to increase our facilities there, so that her possession of the place would hardly be felt by us, and it would not perhaps be very long before some circumstance might arise which might make the cession of it to us the price of something of more worth to her. Not so can it ever be in the hands of France. The impetuosity of her temper, the energy and restlessness of her character, placed in a point of eternal friction with us, and our character, which though quiet, and loving peace & pursuit of wealth, is high-minded, despising wealth in competition with insult or injury, enterprising and energetic as any nation on earth, these circumstances render it impossible that France and the U. S. can continue long friends when they meet in so irritable a position. They as well as we must be blind if they do not see this; and we must be very improvident if we do not begin to make arrangements on that hypothesis . . .

If France considers Louisiana however as indispensable for her views she might perhaps be willing to look about for arrangements which might reconcile it to our interests. If anything could do this it would be the ceding to us the island of New Orleans and the Floridas. This would certainly in a great degree remove the causes of jarring and irritation between us, and perhaps for such a length of time as might produce other means of making the measure permanently conciliatory to our interests and friendships. It would at any rate relieve us from the necessity of taking immediate measures for countervailing such an operation by arrangements in another quarter. Still we should consider N. Orleans and the Floridas as equivalent for the risk of a quarrel with France produced by her vicinage. I have no doubt you have urged these considerations on every proper occasion with the government where you are. They are such as must have effect if you can find the means of producing thorough reflection on them by that government. The idea here is that the troops sent to St. Domingo, were to proceed to Louisiana after finishing their work in that island. If this were the arrangement, it will give you time to return again and again to the charge, for the conquest of St. Domingo will not be a short work. It will take considerable time to wear down a great number of soldiers. Every eye in the U. S. is now fixed on this affair of Louisiana. Perhaps nothing since the revolutionary war has produced more uneasy sensations through the body of the nation. Notwithstanding temporary bickerings have taken place with France, she has still a strong hold on the affections of our citizens generally. I have thought it not amiss, by way of supplement to the letters of the Secretary of State to write you this private one to impress you with the importance we affix to this transaction. I pray you to cherish Dupont. He has the best dispositions for the continuance of friendship between the two nations, and perhaps you may be able to make a good use of him. Accept assurances of my affectionate esteem and high consideration.[6]

To Casper Wister. Washington, February 28, 1803.

Dear Sir—The enclosed sheets may contain some details which may perhaps be thought interesting enough for the transactions of our society. They were forwarded to me by Mr. Dunbar with a couple of vocabularies which I retain to be added to my collection.

What follows is to be perfectly confidential. I have at length succeeded in procuring an essay to be made of exploring the Missouri and whatever river heading with that, runs into the western Ocean. Congress by a secret authority enables me to do it. A party of about 10 chosen men headed by an officer will immediately set out. We cannot in the U. S. find a person who to courage, prudence, habits and health adapted to the woods, and some familiarity with the Indian character, joins a perfect knowledge of botany, natural history, mineralogy and astronomy, all of which would be desirable. To the first qualifications Captain Lewis my Secretary adds a great mass of accurate observation made on the different subjects of the three kingdoms as existing in these states, not under their scientific forms, but so as that he will readily seize whatever is new in the country he passes through, and give us accounts of new things only; and he has qualified himself for fixing the longitude and latitude of the different points in the line he will go over. I have thought it would be useful to confine his attention to those objects only on which information is most deficient and most desireable: and therefore would thank you to make a note on paper of those which occur to you as most desirable for him to attend to. He will be in Philadelphia within two or three weeks and will call on you. Any advice or hints you can give him will be thankfully received and usefully applied. I presume he will complete his tour there and back in two seasons.[7]

To Horatio Gates. Washington, July 11, 1803.

Dear General, I accept with pleasure, and with pleasure reciprocate your congratulations on the acquisition of Louisiana: for it is a subject of mutual congratulations as it interests every man of the nation. The territory acquired, as it includes all the waters of the Missouri and Mississippi, has more than doubled the area of the U. S. and the new part is not inferior of the old in soil, climate, productions and important communications. If our legislature dispose of it with the wisdom we have a right to expect, they may make it the means of tempting all our Indians on the East side of the Mississippi to remove to the West, and of condensing instead of scattering our population. . .

With respect to the territory acquired, I do not think it will be a separate government as you imagine. I presume the island of N. Orleans and the settled country on the opposite bank, will be annexed to the Mississippi territory. We shall certainly endeavor to introduce the American laws there and that cannot be done but by amalgamating the people with such a body of Americans as may take the lead in legislation and government. Of course they will be under the Governor of Mississippi. The rest of the territory will probably be locked up from American settlement, and under the self-government of the native occupants.

You know that every sentence from me is put on the rack by our opponents, to be tortured into something they can make use of. No caution therefore I am sure is necessary against letting my letter go out of your hands.[8]

The Autobiography. July 16, 1803.

The cession of Louisiana being to be ratified by the 30 Oct. shall Congress be called, or only Senate, and when?

Answer unanimous Congress on the 17th of October.

The substance of the treaty to be made public, but not the treaty itself.

The Secretary of State to write to our Consul at N. Orleans, communicating the substance of the treaty and calling his attention to the public property transferred to us, and to archives, papers and documents relative to domain and sovereignty of Louisiana and its dependancies. If an order should come for immediate possession, direct Govr. Claiborne to go and take possn. and act as Governor and Intendant under the Spanish laws, having everything to go on as heretofore, only himself performing functions of Govr. and Intendt. but making no innovation, nor doing a single act which will bear postponing.[9]

To John C. Breckenridge. Monticello, August 12, 1803.

Objections are raising to the Eastward against the vast

extent of our boundaries and propositions are made to exchange Louisiana, or a part of it, for the Floridas. But, as I have said, we shall get the Floridas without, and I would not give one inch of the waters of the Mississippi to any nation, because I see in a light very important to our peace the exclusive right to its navigation, and the admission of no nation into it, but as into the Potomac or Delaware, with our consent and under our police. These federalists see in this acquisition the formation of a new confederacy, embracing all the waters of the Mississippi, on both sides of it, and a separation of its Eastern waters from us.[10]

To John Dickinson. Monticello, August 9, 1803.

Our confederation is certainly confined to the limits established by the revolution. The general government has no powers but such as the constitution has given it; and it has not given it a power of holding foreign territory, and still less of incorporating it into the Union. An amendment of the Constitution seems necessary for this. In the meantime we must ratify and pay our money, as we have treated, for a thing beyond the constitution, and rely on the nation to sanction an act done for its great good, without its previous authority.[11]

To Thomas Paine. August 18, 1803.

Dear Sir—On the 10th inst. I wrote you on the subject of Louisiana, and mentioned the question of a supplement to the constitution on that account. A letter received yesterday renders it prudent to say nothing on that subject, but to do sub-silentio what shall be found necessary. That part of my letter therefore be so good as to consider as confidential.[12]

To the Secretary of State, James Madison.

Monticello, August 18, 1803.

Dear Sir—I enclose you two letters from Rob. R. Livingston. That of the 2d of June is just intelligible enough in the unciphered parts to create anxieties which perhaps the cipher may remove. I communicate them for your information, and shall be glad to receive them deciphered. I infer that the less we say about constitutional difficulties respecting Louisiana the better, and that what is necessary for surmounting them must be done sub-silentio . . .

Mr. King said to Mr. Gallatin that the idea of selling Louisiana was, 4 weeks before the treaty, assimilated at Paris with the sale of Dunkirk by Charles the 2d, and that Mr. Livingston had not at that time the least expectation of success. Accept my affectionate salutations and assurances of constant esteem.[13]

To the Secretary of State, James Madison. Aug. 25, 1803.

I suppose Monroe will touch on the limits of Louisiana only incidentally, inasmuch as its extension to Perdido curtails Florida, and renders it of less worth. I have used my spare moments to investigate, by the help of my books here, the subject of the limits of Louisiana. I am satisfied our right to Perdido is substantial, and can be opposed by a quibble on form only; and our right Westardly to the Bay of St. Bernard, may be strongly maintained. I will use the first leisure to make a statement of the facts and principles on which this depends. Further reflection on the amendment to the Constitution necessary in the case of Louisiana, satisfies me it will be better to give general powers, with specified exceptions, somewhat in the way stated below.[14]

To the Attorney-General. Monticello, August 30, 1803.

. . . The enclosed letter came to hand by yesterday's post. You will be sensible of the circumstances which make it improper that I should hazard a formal answer, as well as of the desire its friendly aspect naturally excites, that those concerned in it should understand that the spirit they express is friendly viewed. You can judge also from your knowledge of the ground, whether it may be usefully encouraged. I take the liberty, therefore, of availing myself of your neighborhood to Boston, and of your friendship to me, to request you to say to the capt. and others verbally whatever you think would be proper, as expressive of my sentiments on the subject. With respect to the day on which they wish to fix their anniversary, they may be told, that disapproving myself of transferring the honors and veneration for the great birthday of our republic to any individual, or of dividing them with individuals, I have declined letting my own birthday be known, and have engaged my family not to communicate it. This has been the uniform answer to every application of the kind.

On further consideration as to the amendment to our Constitution respecting Louisiana, I have thought it better, instead of enumerating the powers which Congress may exercise, to give them the same powers they have as to other portions of the Union generally, and to enumerate the special exceptions, in some such form as the following: . . .

I quote this for your consideration, observing that the less that is said about any constitutional difficulty, the better; and that it will be desirable for Congress to do what is necessary, *in silence....* We meet in Washington the 25th proximo to prepare for Congress. Accept my affectionate salutations and great esteem and respect.[15]

To Wilson Cary Nicholas. Monticello, September 7, 1803.

Dear Sir—Your favor of the 3rd was delivered me at court; but we were much disappointed at not seeing you here, Mr. Madison and the Gov. being here at the time. I enclose you a letter from Monroe on the subject of the late treaty. You will observe a hint in it, to do without delay what we are bound to do. There is reason, in the opinion of our ministers, to believe, that if the thing were to do over again, it could not be obtained, and that if we give the least opening, they will declare the treaty void. A warning amounting to that has been given to them, and an unusual kind of letter written by their minister to our Secretary of State, direct. Whatever Congress shall think it necessary to do, should be done with as little debate as possible, and particularly so far as respects the constitutional difficulty. I am aware of the force of the observations you make on the power given by the Constn. to Congress, to admit new States into the Union, without restraining the subject to the territory then constituting the U. S. But when I consider that the limits of the U. S. are precisely fixed by the treaty of 1783, that the Constitution expressly declares itself to be made for the U. S., I cannot help believing the intention was to permit Congress to admit into the Union new States, which should be formed out of the territory for which, and under whose authority alone, they were then acting. I do not believe it was meant that they might receive England, Ireland, Holland, etc. into it, which would be the case on your construction. When an instrument admits two constructions, the one safe, the other dangerous, the one precise, the other indefinite, I prefer that which is safe and precise. I had rather ask an enlargement of power from the nation, where it is found necessary, than to assume it by a construction which would make our powers boundless. Our peculiar security is in possession of a written Constitution. Let us not make it a blank paper by construction. I say the same as to the opinion of those who consider the grant of the treaty making power as boundless. If it is, then we have no Constitution. If it has bounds, they can be no others than the definitions of the powers which that instrument gives. It specifies and delineates the operations permitted to the federal government, and gives all the powers necessary to carry these into execution. Whatever of these enumerated objects is proper to be executed by way of a treaty, the President and Senate may enter into the treaty; whatever is to be done by a judicial sentence, the judges may pass the sentence. Nothing is more likely than that their enumeration of powers is defective. This is the ordinary case of all human works. Let us go on then perfecting it, by adding, by way of amendment to the Constitution, those powers which time and trial show are still wanting. But it has been taken too much for granted, that by this rigorous construction the treaty power would be reduced to nothing. I had occasion once to examine its effect on the French treaty, made by the old Congress, and found that out of thirty odd articles which that contained, there were one, two, or three only which could not now be stipulated under our present Constitution. I confess, then, I think it important, in the present case, to set an example against broad construction, by appealing for new power to the people. If, however, our friends shall think differently, certainly I shall acquiesce with satisfaction; confiding, that the good sense of our country will correct the evil of construction when it shall produce ill effects.

No apologies for writing or speaking to me freely are necessary. On the contrary, nothing my friends can do is so dear to me, and proves to me their friendship so clearly, as the information they give me of their sentiments and those of others on interesting points where I am to act, and where information and warning is so essential to excite in me that due reflection which ought to precede action. I leave this about the 21st, and shall hope the District Court will give me an opportunity of seeing you.

Accept my affectionate salutations, and assurances of cordial esteem and respect.[16]

To DeWitt Clinton. Washington, December 2, 1803.

. . . I am less able to give you the proceedings of Congress than your correspondents who are of that body. More difference of opinion seems to exist as to the manner of disposing of Louisiana, than I had imagined possible: and our leading friends are not yet sufficiently aware of the necessity of accommodation and mutual sacrifice of opinion for conducting a numerous assembly, where the opposition too is drilled to act in phalanx on every question.

Altho' it is acknowledged that our new fellow citizens are as yet as incapable of self government as children, yet some cannot bring themselves to suspend its principles for a single moment. The temporary or territorial government of that country therefore will encounter great difficulty. The question too whether the settlement of upper Louisiana shall be prohibited occasions a great division of our friends. Some are for prohibiting it till another amendment of the constn shall permit it; others for prohibiting by authority of the legislature only, a third set for permitting immediate settlement. Those of the first opinion apprehend that if the legislature may open a land office there, it will become the ruling principle of elections, and end in a yazoo scheme: those of the 2d opinion fear they may never get an amendment of the constitution permitting settlement.[18]

To James Monroe. Washington, January 8, 1804.

I expect this evening's post will bring us the account that Louisiana was formally delivered to us about the 16th of December. This acquisition is seen by our constituents in all its importance, and they do justice to all those who have been instrumental towards it. Fortunately, the federal leaders have had the imprudence to oppose it pertinaciously, which has given an occasion to a great proportion of their quondam honest adherents to abandon them and join the republican standard. They feel themselves now irretrievably lost, and are ceasing to make further opposition in the states, or anywhere but in Congress. I except however N. Hampshire, Mass. Connect. and Delaware. The 1st will be with us in the course of this year. . .[18]

To C. F. Comte De Volney.

Washington, February 11, 1806.

. . . Our last news of Captn. Lewis was that he had reached the upper part of the Missouri, and had taken horses to cross the Highlands to the Columbia river. He passed the last winter among the Manians 1610 miles above the mouth of the river. So far he had delineated it with as great accuracy as will probably be ever applied to it, as his courses and distances by mensuration were corrected by almost daily observations of latitude and longitude. With his map he sent us specimens or information of the following animals not before known to the northern continent of America. 1. The horns of what is perhaps a species of Ovis Ammon. 2. A variety of the deer having a black tail. 3. An antelope. 4. The badger, not before known out of Europe. 5. A new species of marmotte. 6. A white weasel. 7. The magpie. 8. The Prairie hen, said to resemble the Guinea hen (peintade). 9. A prickly lizard. To these are added a considerable collection of minerals, not yet analyzed. He wintered in Lat. 47° 20′ and found the maximum of cold 43° below the zero of Fahrenheit. We expect he has reached the Pacific, and is now wintering on the head of the Missouri, and will be here next autumn. Having been disappointed in our view of sending an exploring party up the Red river the last year, they were sent up the Washita, as far as the hot springs, under the direction of Mr. Dunbar. He found the temperature of the springs 150° of Fahrenheit and the water perfectly potable when cooled. We obtain also the geography of that river, so far with perfect accuracy. Our party is just at this time setting out from Natchez to ascend the Red river. These expeditions are so laborious, and hazardous, that men of science, used to the temperature and inactivity of their closet, cannot be induced to undertake them. They are headed therefore by persons qualified expressly to give us the geography of the rivers with perfect accuracy, and of good common knowledge and observation in the animal, vegetable and mineral departments. When the route shall be once open and known, scientific men will undertake, and verify and class its subjects. Our emigration to the western country from these states the last year is estimated at about 100,000. I conjecture that about one-half the number of our increase will emigrate westward annually.[19]

To John Dickinson. Washington, January 13, 1807.

My Dear and Ancient Friend—I have duly received your favor of the 1st inst., and am ever thankful for communications which may guide me in the duties which I wish to perform as well as I am able. It is but too true that great discontents exist in the territory of Orleans. Those of the French inhabitants have for their sources, 1. the prohibition of importing slaves. This may be partly removed by Congress permitting them to receive slaves from the other States, which, by dividing that evil, would lessen its danger; 2. the administration of justice in our forms, principles, and language, with all of which they are unacquainted, and are the more abhorrent, because of the enormous expense, greatly exaggerated by the corruption of bankrupt and greedy lawyers, who have gone there from the U. S. and engrossed the practice; 3. the call on them by the land commissioners to produce the titles of their lands. The object of this is really to record and secure their rights. But as many of them hold on rights so ancient that the title papers are lost, they expect the land is to be taken from them wherever they cannot produce a regular deduction of title in writing. In this they will be undeceived by the final result, which will evince to them a liberal disposition of the government towards them. Among the American inhabitants it is the old division of federalists and republicans. The former are as hostile there as they are everywhere, and are the most numerous and wealthy. They have been long endeavoring to batter down the Governor, who has always been a firm republican. There were characters superior to him whom I wished to appoint, but they refused the office: I know no better man who would accept of it, and it would not be right to turn him out for one not better. But it is the 2d. cause, above mentioned, which is deep-seated and permanent. The French members of the Legislature, being the majority in both Houses, lately passed an act declaring that the civil, or French laws, should be the laws of their land, and enumerated about 50 folio volumes, in Latin, as the despositories of these laws. The Governor negatived the act. One of the houses thereupon passed a vote for self-dissolution of the Legislature as a useless body, which failed in the other House by a single vote only. They separated, however, and have disseminated all the discontent they could. I propose to the members of Congress in conversation, the enlisting of 30,000 volunteers, Americans by birth, to be carried at the public expense, and settled immediately on a bounty of 160 acres of land each, on the west side of the Mississippi, on the condition of giving two years of military service, if that country should be attacked within seven years. The defense of the country would thus be placed on the spot, and the additional number would entitle the territory to become a State, would make the majority American, and make it an American instead of a French State. This would not sweeten the pill to the French; but in making that acquisition we had some view to our own good as well as theirs, and I believe the greatest good of both will be promoted by whatever will amalgamate us together.

I have tired you, my friend, with a long letter. But your tedium will end in a few lines more. Mine has yet two years to endure. I am tired of an office where I can do no more good than many others, who would be glad to be employed in it. To myself, personally, it brings nothing but unceasing drudgery and daily loss of friends. Every office becoming vacant, every appointment made, *me donne un ingrat, et cent ennemis.* My only consolation is in the belief that my fellow citizens at large give me credit for good intentions. I will certainly endeavor to merit the continuance of that good-will which follows well-intended actions, and their approbation will be the dearest reward I can carry into retirement.

God bless you, my excellent friend, and give you yet many healthy and happy years.[20]

To James Monroe. Monticello, February 4, 1816.

A propos, of the dispute with Spain, as to the boundary of Louisiana. On our acquisition of that country, there was found in possession of the family of the late Governor Messier, a most valuable and original MS. history of the settlement of Louisiana by the French, written by Bernard de la Harpe, a principal agent through the whole of it. It commences with the first permanent settlement of 1699, (that by de la Salle in 1684, having been broken up.) and continues to 1723, and shows clearly the continual claim of France to the Province of Texas, as far as the Rio Bravo, and to all the waters running into the Mississippi, and how, by the roguery of St. Denis, an agent of Crozat, the merchant, to whom the colony was granted for ten years, the settlement of the Spaniards at Nacadoches, Adais, Assinays, and Natchitoches, were fraudulently invited and connived at. Crozat's object was commerce, and especially contraband, with the Spaniards, and these posts were settled as convenient smuggling stages on the way to Mexico. The history bears such marks of authenticity as place it beyond question. Governor Claiborne obtained the MS. for us, and thinking it too hazardous to risk its loss by the way, unless a copy were retained, he had a copy taken. The original having arrived safe at Washington, he sent me the copy, which I now have. Is the original still in your office? Or was it among the papers burnt by the British? If lost, I will send you my copy; if preserved, it is my wish to deposit the copy for safe keeping with the Philosophical Society at Philadelphia, where it will be safer than on my shelves. I do not mean that any part of this letter shall give to yourself the trouble of an answer; only desire Mr. Graham to see if the original still exists in your office, and to drop me a line saying yea or nay; and I shall know what to do. Indeed the MS. ought to be printed, and I see a note to my copy which shows it has been in contemplation, and that it was computed to be of twenty sheets at sixteen dollars a sheet, for three hundred and twenty copies, which would sell at one dollar apiece, and reimburse the expense . . .[21]

To Albert Gallatin. Monticello, November 24, 1818.

Dear Sir—Your letter of July 22 was most acceptable to me, by the distinctness of the view it presented of the state of France. I rejoice in the prospect that that country will so soon recover from the effects of the depression under which it has been laboring; and especially I rejoice in the hope of its enjoying a government as free as perhaps the state of things will yet bear. It appears to me, indeed, that their constitution, as it now is, gives them a legislative branch more equally representative, more independent, and certainly of more integrity, than the corresponding one in England. Time and experience will give what is still wanting, and I hope they will wait patiently for that without hazarding new convulsions.

Here all is well. The President's message, delivered a few days ago, will have given you a correct view of the state of our affairs. The capture of Pensacola, which furnished so much speculation for European news-writers (who imagine that our political code, like theirs, had no chapter of morality), was nothing here. In the first moment, indeed, there was a general out-cry of condemnation of what appeared to be a wrongful aggression. But this was quieted at once by information that it had been taken without orders and would be instantly restored; and although done without orders, yet not without justifiable cause, as we are assured will be satisfactorily shown. This manifestation of the will of our citizens to countenance no injustice towards a foreign nation filled me with comfort as to our future course.

Emigration to the West and South is going on beyond anything imaginable. The President told me lately that the sales of public lands within the last year would amount to ten millions of dollars. There is only one passage in his message which I disapprove, and which I trust will not be approved by our legislature. It is that which proposes to subject the Indians to our laws without their consent. A little patience and a little money are so rapidly producing their voluntary removal across the Mississippi, that I hope this immorality will not be permitted to stain our history. He has certainly been surprised into this proposition, so little in concord with our principles of government.

My strength has been sensibly declining the last few years, and my health greatly broken by an illness of three months, from which I am but now recovering. I have been able to get on horseback within these three or four days, and trust that my convalescence will now be steady. I am able to write you a letter on the subject of my friend Cathalan, a very intimate friend of three and thirty years' standing, and a servant of the United States of near forty years. I am aware that his office is coveted by another, and suppose it possible that intrigue may have been employed to get him removed. But I know him too well not to pronounce him incapable of such misconduct as ought to overweigh the long course of his services to the United States. I confess I should feel with great sensibility a disgrace inflicted on him at this period of life. But on this subject I must write to you more fully when I shall have more strength, for as yet I sit at the writing table with great pain.

I am obliged to usurp the protection of your cover for my letters—a trouble, however, which will be rare hereafter. My package is rendered more bulky on this occasion by a book I transmit for M. Tracy. It is a translation of his *Economie politique,* which we have made and published here in the hope of advancing our countrymen somewhat in that science; the most profound ignorance of which threatened irreparable disaster during the late war, and by the parasite institutions of banks is now consuming the public industry. The flood with which they are deluging us of nominal money has placed us completely without any certain measure of value, and, by interpolating a false measure, is deceiving and ruining multitudes of our citizens.[22]

To Joseph C. Cabell. Monticello, January 22, 1820.

Dear Sir—I send you the inclosed as an exhibit to our enemies as well as friends. Kentucky, our daughter, planted since Virginia was a distinguished state, has an University, with 14 professors and upwards of 200 students. While we, with a fund of a million and a half of Dollars ready raised and appropriated, are higgling without the heart to let it go to its use. If our legislature does not heartily push our University, we must send our children for education to Kentucky or Cambridge. The latter will return them to us fanatics and tories, the former will keep them to add to their population. If however we are to go a begging anywhere for our education, I would rather it should be to Kentucky than any other state, because she has more of the flavor of the old cask than any other. All the states but our own are sensible that knowledge is power. The Missouri question is for power. The efforts now generally making all the states to advance their science is for power, while we are sinking into the barbarism of our Indian aborigines, and expect like them to oppose by ignorance the overwhelming mass of light and science by which we shall be surrounded. It is a comfort that I am not to live to see this. Our exertions in building this last year have amounted to the whole of the public annuity of this year, for which therefore we have been obliged to draw to relieve the actual distresses of our workmen; the subscriptions come in slow and grudgingly. You know that we are to pay Dr. Cooper 1500 D. in May, and his family will depend on it for subsistence in his absence. We have been obliged therefore to set apart, as our only sure dependence, six subscriptions on the punctuality of which we can depend, to wit, yours, Mr. Madison's, Genl. Cocke's, Mr. Diges's and John Harrison's and mine, which exactly make up the money. Affectionately yours.[23]

The importance of domestic manufacturing, rational approaches to public debt and financial crises and the impact of international piracy threatening "to keep us in eternal vassalage to a foreign and unfriendly people" are the subjects of this series of letters.

On the Economy

To James Monroe. Monticello, September 24, 1814.

Dear Sir—The events which have lately taken place at Washington, and which truly disgrace our enemies much more than us, have occupied you too much to admit intrusions by private and useless letters. You seem indeed to have had your hands full with the duties of the field and the double duties of the Cabinet. The success of McDonough has been happily timed to dispel the gloom of your present meeting, and to open the present session of Congress with hope and good humor. To add however to our embarrassments, it happens to be the moment when the general bankruptcy comes upon us, which has been so long and so certainly impending. The banks declare they will not pay their bills which is sufficiently understood to mean that they cannot. Although this truth has been long expected, yet their own declaration was wanting to fix the moment of insolvency. Their paper is now offered doubtingly, received by some merely from the total absence of all other medium of payment, and absolutely rejected by others; and in no case will a half-disme of cash be given in change. The annihilation of these institutions has come on us suddenly therefore, which I had thought should be suppressed, but gradatim only, in order to prevent, as much as possible, the crush of private fortunes.

This catastrophe happening just as our legislature was about to meet . . .[1]

To James Monroe. Monticello, January 1, 1815.

Although a century of British experience has proved to what a wonderful extent the funding on specific redeeming taxes enables a nation to anticipate in war the resources of peace, and although the other nations of Europe have tried and trodden every path of force or folly in fruitless quest of the same object, yet we still expect to find in juggling tricks and banking dreams, that money can be made out of nothing, and in sufficient quantity to meet the expenses of a heavy war by sea and land. It is said, indeed, that money cannot be borrowed from our merchants as from those of England. But it can be borrowed from our people. They will give you all the necessaries of war they produce, if, instead of the bankrupt trash they are now obliged to receive for want of any other, you will give them a paper promise funded on a specific pledge, and of a size for common circulation. But you say the merchants will not take this paper. What the people take the merchants must take or sell nothing. All these doubts and fears prove only the extent of the dominion which the banking institutions have obtained over the minds of our citizens, and especially of those inhabiting cities or other banking places; and this dominion must be broken, or it will break us. But here, as in the other case, we must make up our minds to suffer yet longer before we can get right. The misfortune is, that in the meantime we shall plunge ourselves in unextinguishable debt, and entail on our posterity an inheritance of eternal taxes, which will bring our government and people into the condition of those of England, a nation of pikes and gudgeons, the latter bred merely as food for the former.[2]

To Benjamin Austin. Monticello, January 9, 1816.

You tell me I am quoted by those who wish to continue our dependence on England for manufactures. There was a time when I might have been so quoted with more candor, but within the thirty years which have since elapsed, how are circumstances changed! We were then in peace. Our independent place among nations was acknowledged. A commerce which offered the raw material in exchange for the same material after receiving the last touch of industry, was worthy of welcome to all nations. It was expected that those especially to whom manufacturing industry was important, would cherish the friendship of such customers by every favor, by every inducement, and particularly cultivate their peace by every act of justice and friendship. Under this prospect the question seemed legitimate, whether, with such an immensity of unimproved land, courting the hand of husbandry, the industry of agriculture, or that of manufactures, would add most to the national wealth? And the doubt was entertained on this consideration chiefly, that to the labor of the husbandman a vast addition is made by the spontaneous energies of the earth on which it is employed: for one grain of wheat committed to the earth, she renders twenty, thirty, and even fifty fold, whereas to the labor of the manufacturer nothing is added. Pounds of flax, in his hands, yield, on the contrary, but pennyweights of lace. This exchange, too, laborious as it might seem, what a field did it promise for the occupations of the ocean; what a nursery for that class of citizens who were to exercise and maintain our equal rights on that element? This was the state of things in 1785, when the "Notes on Virginia" were first printed; when, the ocean being open to all nations, and their common right in it acknowledged and exercised under regulations sanctioned by the assent and usage of all, it was thought that the doubt might claim some consideration. But who in 1785 could foresee the rapid depravity which was to render the close of that century the disgrace of the history of man? Who could have imagined that the two most distinguished in the rank of nations, for science and civilization, would have suddenly descended from that honorable eminence, and setting at defiance all those moral laws established by the Author of nature between nation and nation, as between man and man, would cover earth and sea with robberies and piracies, merely because strong enough to do it with temporal impunity; and that under this disbandment of nations from social order, we should have been despoiled of a thousand ships, and have thousands of our citizens reduced to Algerine slavery. Yet all this has taken place. One of these nations interdicted to our vessels all harbors of the globe without having first proceeded to some one of hers, there paid a tribute proportioned to the cargo, and obtained her license to proceed to the port of destination. The other declared them to be lawful prize if they had touched at the port, or been visited by a ship of the enemy nation. Thus were we completely excluded from the ocean. Compare this state of things with that of '85, and say whether an opinion founded in the circumstances of that day can be fairly applied to those of the present. We have experienced what we did not then believe, that there exists both profligacy and power enough to exclude us from the field of interchange with other nations: that to be independent for the comforts of life we must fabricate them ourselves. . . . If it shall be proposed to go beyond our own supply, the question of '85 will then recur, will our *surplus* labor be then most beneficially employed in the culture of the earth, or in the fabrications of art? We have time yet for consideration, before that question will press upon us; and the maxim to be applied will depend on the circumstances which shall then exist; for in so complicated a science as political economy, no one axiom can be laid down as wise and expedient for all times and circumstances, and for their contraries. Inattention to this is what has called for this explanation, which reflection would have rendered unnecessary with the candid, while nothing will do it with those who use the former opinion only as a stalking horse, to cover their disloyal propensities to keep us in eternal vassalage to a foreign and unfriendly people.[3]

To Richard Rush. Monticello, June 22, 1819.

Dear Sir—Your favor of March 1 has been duly received, and requires my thanks for the kind offer of your services in London. Books are indeed with me a necessary of life; and since I ceded my library to Congress, I have been annually importing from Paris. Not but that I need some from London also, but that they have risen there to such enormous prices as cannot be looked at. England must lose her foreign commerce in books, unless the taxes on its materials are reduced. Paris now prints the most popular of the English books, and sells them far below the English price. I send there therefore for such of them as I want. We too reprint now such of the new English works as have merit, much cheaper than is done in England, but dearer than they ought to be. But we are now under the operation of the remedy for that. The enormous abuses of the banking system are not only prostrating our commerce, but producing revolution of property, which without more wisdom than we possess, will be much greater than were produced by the revolutionary paper. That too had the merit of purchasing our liberties, while the present trash has only furnished aliment to usurers and swindlers. The banks themselves were doing business on capitals, three fourths of which were fictitious; and, to extend their profit they furnished fictitious capital to every man, who having nothing and disliking the labours of the plough, chose rather to call himself a merchant to set up a house of 5000 D. a year expence to dash into every species of mercantile gambling, and if that ended as gambling generally does, a fraudulent bankruptcy was an ultimate resource of retirement and competence. This fictitious capital, probably of 100 millions of Dollars, is now to be lost, and to fall on some body; it must take on those who have property to meet it, and probably on the less cautious part, who, not aware of the impending catastrophe have suffered themselves to contract, or to be in debt, and must now sacrifice their property of a value many times the amount of their debt. We have been truly sowing the wind, and are now reaping the whirlwind. If the present crisis should end in the annihilation of these pennyless and ephemeral interlopers only, and reduce our commerce to the measure of our own wants and surplus productions, it will be a benefit in the end. But how to effect this, and give time to real capital, and the holders of real property, to back out of their entanglements by degrees requires more knowledge of Political economy than we possess. I believe it might be done, but I despair of its being done. The eyes of our citizens are not yet sufficiently open to the true cause of our distresses. They ascribe them to every thing but their true cause, the banking system; a system, which, if it could do good in any form, is yet so certain of leading to abuse, as to be utterly incompatible with the public safety and prosperity. At present all is confusion, uncertainty and panic . . .[4]

To Hugh Nelson. Monticello. February 7, 1820.

I observe you are loaded with petitions from the Manu-facturing commercial and agricultural interests, each pray-ing you to sacrifice the others to them. This proves the egotism of the whole and happily balances their cannibal appetites to eat one another. The most perfect confidence in the wisdom of Congress leaves me without a fear of the result. I do not know whether it is any part of the petitions of the farmers that our citizens shall be restrained to eat nothing but bread, because that can be made here. But this is the common spirit of all their petitions. My ill-health has obliged me to retire from all public concerns. I scarcely read a newspaper. I cannot therefore tell you what is a doing in the state, but this you will get fully from others.[5]

To Hugh Nelson. Monticello, March 12, 1820.

This State is in a condition of unparalleled distress.

The sudden reduction of the circulating medium from a plethory to all but annihilation is producing an entire revolution of fortune. In other places I have known lands sold by the sheriff for one year's rent; beyond the mountain we hear of good slaves selling for one hundred dollars, good horses for five dollars, and the sheriffs generally the purchasers. Our produce is now selling at market for one-third of its price, before this commercial catastrophe, say flour at three and a quarter and three and a half dollars the barrel. We should have less right to expect relief from our legislators if they had been the establishers of the unwise system of banks. A remedy to a certain degree was practicable, that of reducing the quantum of circulation gradually to a level with that of the countries with which we have commerce, and an eternal abjuration of paper. But they have adjourned without doing anything. I fear local insurrections against these horrible sacrifices of property.[6]

To Albert Gallatin. Monticello, December 26, 1820.

At home things are not well. The flood of paper money, as you well know, had produced an exaggeration of nominal prices, and at the same time a facility of obtaining money, which not only encouraged speculations on fictitious capital, but seduced those of real capital, even in private life, to contract debts too freely. Had things continued in the same course, these might have been manageable: but the operations of the United States Bank for the demolition of the States banks obliged these suddenly to call in more than half of their paper, crushed all fictitious and doubtful capital, and reduced the prices of property and produce suddenly to one-third of what they had been. Wheat, for example, at the distance of two or three days from market, fell to, and continued at, from one-third to half a dollar. Should it be stationary at this for a while, a very general revolution of property must take place. Something of the same character has taken place in our fiscal system. A little while back, Congress seemed at a loss for objects whereon to squander the supposed fathomless fund of our Treasury. This short frenzy has been arrested by a deficit of 5 millions the last year and of 7 millions this year. A loan was adopted for the former and is proposed for the latter, which threatens to saddle us with a perpetual debt. I hope a tax will be preferred, because it will awaken the attention of the people and make reformation and economy the principles of the next election. The frequent recurrence of this chastening operation can alone restrain the propensity of governments to enlarge expense beyond income. . . .[7]

Four long and detailed letters on Republican government and the Constitution.

Government and the Constitution

To Samuel Kercheval. Monticello, July 12, 1816.

I duly received your favor of June the 13th, with the copy of the letters on the calling a convention, on which you are pleased to ask my opinion. I have not been in the habit of mysterious reserve on any subject, nor of buttoning up my opinions within my own doublet. On the contrary, while in public service especially, I thought the public entitled to frankness, and intimately to know whom they employed . . . The question you propose, on equal representation, has become a party one, in which I wish to take no public share. Yet, if it be asked for your own satisfaction only, and not to be quoted before the public, I have no motive to withhold it, and the less from you, as it coincides with your own. At the birth of our republic, I committed that opinion to the world, in the draught of a constitution annexed to the "Notes on Virginia," in which a provision was inserted for a representation permanently equal. The infancy of the subject at that moment, and our inexperience of self-government, occasioned gross departures in that draught from genuine republican canons. In truth, the abuses of monarchy had so much filled all the space of political contemplation, that we imagined everything republican which was not monarchy. We had not yet penetrated to the mother principle, that "governments are republican only in proportion as they embody the will of their people, and execute it." Hence, our first constitutions had really no leading principles in them. But experience and reflection have but more and more confirmed me in the particular importance of the equal representation then proposed. On that point, then, I am entirely in sentiment with your letters; and only lament that a copy-right of your pamphlet prevents their appearance in the newspapers, where alone they would be generally read, and produce general effect. The present vacancy too, of other matter, would give them place in every paper, and bring the question home to every man's conscience.

But inequality of representation in both Houses of our legislature, is not the only republican heresy in this first essay of our revolutionary patriots at forming a constitution. For let it be agreed that a government is republican in proportion as every member composing it has his equal voice in the direction of its concerns (not indeed in person, which would be impracticable beyond the limits of a city, or small township, but) by representatives chosen by himself, and responsible to him at short periods, and let us bring to the test of this canon every branch of our constitution.

In the legislature, the House of Representatives is chosen by less than half the people, and not at all in proportion to those who do choose. The Senate are still more disproportionate, and for long terms of irresponsibility. In the Executive, the Governor is entirely independent of the choice of the people, and of their control; his council equally so, and at best but a fifth wheel to a wagon. In the Judiciary, the judges of the highest courts are dependent on none but themselves. In England, where judges were named and removable at the will of an hereditary executive, from which branch most misrule was feared, and has flowed, it was a great point gained, by fixing them for life, to make them independent of that executive. But in a government founded on the public will, this principle operates in an opposite direction, and against that will. There, too, they were still removable on a concurrence of the executive and legislative branches. But we have made them independent of the nation itself. They are irremovable, but by their own body, for any depravities of conduct, and even by their own body for the imbecilities of dotage. The justices of the inferior courts are self-chosen, are for life, and perpetuate their own body in succession forever, so that a faction once possessing themselves of the bench of a county, can never be broken up, but hold their county in chains, forever indissoluble. Yet these justices are the real executive as well as judiciary, in all our minor and most ordinary concerns. They tax us at will; fill the office of sheriff, the most important of all the executive officers of the county; name nearly all our military leaders, which leaders, once named, are removable but by themselves. The juries, our judges of all fact, and of law when they choose it, are not selected by the people, nor amenable to them. They are chosen by an officer named by the court and executive. Chosen, did I say? Picked up by the sheriff from the loungings of the court yard, after everything respectable has retired from it. Where then is our republicanism to be found? Not in our constitution certainly, but merely in the spirit of our people. That would oblige even a despot to govern us republicanly. Owing to this spirit, and to nothing in the form of our constitution, all things have gone well. But this fact, so triumphantly misquoted by the reformation, is not the fruit of our constitution, but has prevailed in spite of it. Our functionaries have done well, because generally honest men. If any were not so, they feared to show it.

But it will be said, it is easier to find faults than to amend them. I do not think their amendment so difficult as it pretended. Only lay down true principles, and adhere to them inflexibly. Do not be frightened into their surrender by the alarms of the timid, or the croakings of wealth against the ascendency of the people. If experience be called for, appeal to that of our fifteen or twenty governments for forty years, and show me where the people have done half the mischief in these forty years, that a single despot would have done in a single year; or show half the riots and rebellions, the crimes and the punishments, which have taken place in any single nation, under kingly government during the same period. The true foundation of republican government is the equal right of every citizen, in his person and property, and in their management. Try by this, as a tally, every provision of our constitution, and see if it hangs directly on the will of the people. Reduce your legislature to a convenient number for full, but orderly discussion. Let every man who fights or pays, exercise his just and equal right in their election. Submit them to approbation or rejection at short intervals. Let the executive be chosen in the same way, and for the same term, by those whose agent he is to be; and leave no screen of a council behind which to skulk from responsibility. It has been thought that the people are not competent electors of judges *learned in the law*. But I do not know that this is true, and, if doubtful we should follow principle. In this, as in many other elections they would be guided by reputation, which would not err oftener, perhaps, than the present mode of appointment. In one State of the Union, at least, it has long been tried, and with the most satisfactory success. The judges of Connecticut have been chosen by the people every six months, for nearly two centuries, and I believe there has hardly ever been an instance of change; so powerful is the curb of incessant responsibility. If prejudice, however, derived from a monarchial institution, is still to prevail against the vital elective principle of our own, and if the existing example among ourselves of periodical election of judges by the people be still mistrusted, let us at least not adopt the evil and reject the good of the English precedent; let us retain removability on the concurrence of the executive and legislative branches, and nomination by the executive alone. Nomination to office is an executive function. To give it to the legislature, as we do, is a violation of the principle of the separation of powers. It swerves the members from correctness, by temptations to intrigue for office themselves, and to a corrupt barter of votes; and destroys responsibility by dividing it among a multitude. By leaving nomination in its proper place, among executive functions, the principle of the distribution of power is preserved, and responsibility weighs with its heaviest force on a single head . . .

I have thrown out these as loose heads of amendment, for consideration and correction; and their object is to

secure self-government by the republicanism of our constitution, as well as by the spirit of the people; and to nour-
ish and perpetuate that spirit. I am not among those who
fear the people. They, and not the rich, are our dependence for continued freedom. And to preserve their independence, we must not let our rulers load us with perpetual
debt. We must make our election between *economy and
liberty, or profusion and servitude.* If we run into such
debts, as that we must be taxed in our meat and in our
drink, in our necessaries and our comforts, in our labors
and our amusements, for our callings and our creeds, as
the people of England are, our people, like them, must
come to labor sixteen hours in the twenty-four, give the
earnings of fifteen of these to the government for their
debts and daily expenses; and the sixteenth being insuffi-
cient to afford us bread, we must live, as they now do, on
oatmeal and potatoes; have no time to think, no means of
calling the mismanagers to account; but be glad to obtain
subsistence by hiring ourselves to rivet their chains on the
necks of our fellow-sufferers. Our landholders, too, like
theirs, retaining indeed the title and stewardship of estates
called theirs, but held really in trust for the treasury, must
wander, like theirs, in foreign countries, and be contented
with penury, obscurity, exile, and the glory of the nation.
This example reads to us the salutary lesson, that private
fortunes are destroyed by public as well as by private ex-
travagance. And this is the tendency of all human governments. A departure from principle in one instance becomes
a precedent for a second; that second for a third; and so
on, till the bulk of the society is reduced to mere automa-
tons of misery, and to have no sensibilities left but for sin-

ning and suffering. Then begins, ideed, the *bellum omnium in omnia,* which some philosophers observing to be so general in this world, have mistaken it for the natural, instead of the abusive state of man. And the fore horse of this frightful team is public debt. Taxation follows that, and in its train wretchedness and oppression.

Some men look at constitutions with sanctimonius reverence, and deem them like the arc of the covenant, too sacred to be touched. They ascribe to the men of the preceding age a wisdom more than human, and suppose what they did to be beyond amendment. I knew that age well; I belonged to it, and labored with it. It deserved well of its country. It was very like the present, but without the experience of the present; and forty years of experience in government is worth a century of book-reading; and this they would say themselves, were they to rise from the dead. I am certainly not an advocate for frequent and untried changes in laws and constitutions. I think moderate imperfections had better be borne with; because, when once known, we accommodate ourselves to them, and find practical means of correcting their ill effects. But I know also, that laws and institutions must go hand in hand with the progress of the human mind. As that becomes more developed, more enlightened, as new discoveries are made, new truths disclosed, and manners and opinions change with the change of circumstances, institutions must advance also, and keep pace with the times. We might as well require a man to wear still the coat which fitted him when a boy, as civilized society to remain ever under the regimen of their barbarous ancestors. It is this preposterous idea which has lately deluged Europe in blood. Their monarchs, instead of wisely yielding to the gradual change of circumstances, of favoring progressive accommodation to progressive improvement, have clung to old abuses, entrenched themselves behind steady habits, and obliged their subjects to seek through blood and violence rash and ruinous innovations, which, had they been referred to the peaceful deliberations and collected wisdom of the nation, would have been put into acceptable and salutary forms. Let us follow no such examples, nor weakly believe that one generation is not as capable as another of taking care of itself, and of ordering its own affairs . . .[1]

To Samuel Kercheval. Monticello, September 5, 1816.

I am glad to see that the Staunton meeting has rejected the idea of a limited convention. The article, however, nearest my heart, is the division of counties into wards. These will be pure and elementary republics, the sum of all which, taken together, composes the State, and will make of the whole a true democracy as to the business of the wards, which is that of nearest and daily concern. The affairs of the larger sections, of counties, of States, and of the Union, not admitting personal transaction by the people, will be delegated to agents elected by themselves; and representation will thus be substituted, where personal action becomes impracticable. Yet, even over these representative organs, should they become corrupt and perverted, the division into wards constituting the people, in their wards, a regularly organized power, enables them by that organization to crush, regularly and peaceably, the usurpations of their unfaithful agents, and rescues them from the dreadful necessity of doing it insurrectionally. In this way we shall be as republican as a large society can be; and secure the continuance of purity in our government, by the salutary, peaceable, and regular control of the people. No other depositories of power have ever yet been found, which did not end in converting to their own profit the earnings of those committed to their charge. George the III. in execution of the trust confided to him, has, within his own day, loaded the inhabitants of Great Britain with debts equal to the whole fee-simple value of their island, and under pretext of governing it, has alienated its whole soil to creditors who could lend money to be lavished on priests, pensions, plunder and perpetual war. This would not have been so, had the people retained organized means of acting on their agents. In this example, then, let us read a lesson for ourselves, and not "go and do likewise."[2]

To William Johnson. Monticello, October 27, 1822.

What do you think of the state of parties at this time? An opinion prevails that there is no longer any distinction, that the republicans and federalists are completely amalgamated but it is not so. The amalgamation is of name only, not of principle. All indeed call themselves by the name of Republicans, because that of Federalists was extinguished in the battle of New Orleans. But the truth is that finding that monarchy is a desperate wish in this country, they rally to the point which they think next best, a consolidated government. Their aim is now therefore to break down the rights reserved by the constitution to the states as a bulwark against that consolidation, the fear of which produced the whole of the opposition to the constitution at its birth. Hence new Republicans in Congress, preaching the doctrines of the old Federalists, and the new nick-names of Ultras and Radicals. But I trust they will fail under the new, as the old name, and that the friends of the real constitution and union will prevail against consolidation, as they have done against monarchism. I scarcely know myself which is most to be deprecated, a consolidation, or dissolution of the states. The horrors of both are beyond the reach of human foresight.[3]

To William Johnson. Monticello, June 12, 1823.

Dear Sir—Our correspondence is of that accommodating character, which admits of suspension at the convenience of either party, without inconvenience to the other. Hence this tardy acknowledgement of your favor of April the 11th. I learned from that with great pleasure, that you have resolved on continuing your history of parties. Our opponents are far ahead of us in preparations for placing their cause favorably before posterity. Yet I hope even from some of them the escape of precious truths, in angry explosions or effusions of vanity, which will betray the genuine monarchism of their principles. They do not themselves believe what they endeavor to inculcate, that we were an opposition party, not on principle, but merely seeking for office. The fact is, that at the formation of our government, many had formed their political opinions on European writings and practices, believing the experience of old countries, and especially of England, abusive as it was, to be a safer guide than mere theory. The doctrines of Europe were, that men in numerous associations cannot be restrained within the limits of order and justice, but by

forces physical and moral, wielded over them by authorities independent of their will. Hence their organization of
kings, hereditary nobles, and priests. Still further to con-
strain the brute force of the people, they deem it necessary
to keep them down by hard labor, poverty and ignorance,
and to take from them, as from bees, so much of their
earnings, as that unremitting labor shall be necessary to
obtain a sufficient surplus barely to sustain a scanty and
miserable life. And these earnings they apply to maintain
their privileged orders in splendor and idleness, to fascinate
the eyes of the people, and excite in them an humble ador-
ation and submission, as to an order of superior beings.
Although few among us had gone all these lengths of opinion, yet many had advanced, some more, some less, on the
way. And in the convention which formed our government,
they endeavored to draw the cords of power as tight as
they could obtain them, to lessen the dependence of the
general functionaries on their constituents, to subject to
them those of the States, and to weaken their means of
maintaining the steady equilibrium which the majority of
the convention had deemed salutary for both branches,
general and local. To recover, therefore, in practice the
powers which the nation had refused, and to warp to their
own wishes those actually given, was the steady object of
the federal party. Ours, on the contrary, was to maintain
the will of the majority of the convention, and of the people themselves. We believed, with them, that man was a
rational animal, endowed by nature with rights, and with
an innate sense of justice; and that he could be restrained
from wrong and protected in right, by moderate powers,
confided to persons of his own choice, and held to their

duties by dependence on his own will. We believed that the complicated organization of kings, nobles, and priests, was not the wisest nor best to effect the happiness of associated man; that wisdom and virtue were not hereditary; that the trappings of such a machinery, consumed by their expense, those earnings of industry, they were meant to protect; and, by the inequalities they produced, exposed liberty to sufferance. We believed that man, enjoying in ease and security the full fruits of their own industry, enlisted by all the interests on the side of law and order, habituated to think for themselves, and to follow their reason as their guide, would be more easily and safely governed, than with minds nourished in error, and vitiated and debased, as in Europe, by ignorance, indigence and oppression. The cherishment of the people then was our principle, the fear and distrust of them, that of the other party. Composed, as we were, of the landed and laboring interests of the country, we could not be less anxious for a government of law and order than were the inhabitants of the cities, the strongholds of federalism. And whether our efforts to save the principles and form of our constitution have not been salutary, let the present republican freedom, order and prosperity of our country determine. History may distort truth, and will distort it for a time, by the superior efforts at justification of those who are conscious of needing it most. Nor will the opening scenes of our present government be seen in their true aspect, until the letters of the day, now held in private hoards, shall be broken up and laid open to public view. What a treasure will be found in General Washington's cabinet, when it shall pass into the hands of as candid a friend to truth as he was himself! When no longer, like Caesar's notes and memorandums in the hands of Anthony, it shall be open to the high priests of federalism only, and garbled to say so much, and no more, as suits their views!

With respect to his farewell address, to the authorship of which, it seems, there are conflicting claims, I can state to you some facts. He had determined to decline re-election at the end of his first term, and so far determined, that he had requested Mr. Madison to prepare for him something valedictory, to be addressed to his constituents on his retirement. This was done, but he was finally persuaded to acquiesce in a second election, to which no one more strenuously pressed him than myself, from a conviction of the importance of strengthening, by longer habit, the respect necessary for that office, which the weight of his character only could effect. When, at the end of his second term, his Valedictory came out, Mr. Madison recognized in it several passages of his draught, several others, we were both satisfied, were from the pen of Hamilton, and others from that of the President himself. These he probably put into the hands of Hamilton to form into a whole, and hence it may all appear in Hamilton's hand-writing, as if it were all of his composition.

I have stated above, that the original objects of the federalists were, 1st, to warp our government more to the form and principles of monarchy, and 2d, to weaken the barriers of the State governments as coordinate powers. In the first they have been so completely foiled by the universal spirit of the nation, that they have abandoned the enterprise, shrunk from the odium of their old appellation, taken to themselves a participation of ours, and under the pseudo-republican mask, are now aiming at their second object, and strengthened by unsuspecting or apostate recruits from our ranks, are advancing fast towards an ascendancy. I have been blamed for saying, that a prevalence of the doctrines of consolidation would one day call for reformation or *revolution*. I answer by asking if a single State of the Union would have agreed to the constitution, had it given all powers to the General Government? If the whole opposition to it did not proceed from the jealousy and fear of every State, of being subjected to the other States in matters merely its own? And if there is any reason to believe the States more disposed now than then, to acquiesce in this general surrender of all their rights and powers to a consolidated government, one and undivided?[4]

Jefferson's comments on some of his contemporaries including James Madison, Hamilton, John Adams, George Washington and Aaron Burr, appear in the following letters with long retrospective notes on the revolution and the War of 1812.

Party Leaders and the Revolution

To George Washington. Paris, May 2, 1788.

Sir—I am honored with your Excellency's letter by the last packet and thank you for the information it contains on the communication between the Cayahoga and Big Beaver. I have ever considered the opening a canal between those two water courses as the most important work in that line which the state of Virginia could undertake. It will infallibly turn through the Potomac all the commerce of Lake Erie and the country west of that, except what may pass down the Mississippi, and it is important that it be soon done, lest that commerce should in the mean time get established in another channel. Having in the spring of last year taken a journey through the Southern parts of France, and particularly examined the canal of Languedoc through its whole course, I take the liberty of sending you the notes I made on the spot, as you may find in them something perhaps which may be turned to account some time or other in the prosecution of the Potomac canal. Being merely a copy from my notes they are undigested and imperfect, but may still perhaps give hints capable of improvement in your mind. . . .

I had intended to have written a word to your Excellency on the subject of the new constitution, but I have already spun out my letter to an immoderate length. I will just observe therefore that according to my ideas there is a great deal of good in it. There are two things however which I dislike strongly. 1. The want of a declaration of rights. I am in the hopes the opposition of Virginia will remedy this and produce such a declaration. 2. The perpetual re-eligibility of the President. This I fear will make an office for life first, and then hereditary. I was much an enemy to monarchy before I came to Europe. I am ten thousand times more so since I have seen what they are. There is scarcely an evil known in these countries which may not be traced to their king as its source, nor a good which is not derived from the small fibres of republicanism existing among them. I can further say with safety there is not a crowned head in Europe whose talents or merit would entitle him to be elected a vestryman by the people of any parish in America. However I shall hope that before there is danger of this change taking place in the office of President, the good sense and free spirit of our countrymen will make the changes necessary to prevent it. Under this hope I look forward to the general adoption of the new constitution with anxiety as necessary for us under our present circumstances.[1]

Anas. 1791.

But Hamilton was not only a monarchist but for a monarchy bottomed on corruption. In proof of this, I will relate an anecdote for the truth of which I attest the God who made me. Before the President set out on his Southern tour in April, 1791, he addressed a letter of the fourth of that month, from Mount Vernon, to the Secretaries of State, Treasury, and War, desiring that if any serious and important cases should arise during his absence they would consult and act on them. And he requested that the Vice-President should also be consulted. This was the only occasion in which that officer was ever requested to take part in a Cabinet question. Some occasions for consultation arising, I invited these gentlemen (and the Attorney-General, as well as I remember) to dine with me, in order to confer on the subject. After the cloth was removed, and our question was agreed and dismissed, conversation began on other matters, and by some circumstance was let to the British Constitution on which Mr. Adams observed, "purge that Constitution of its corruption, and give to its popular branch equality of representation, and it would be the most perfect Constitution ever devised by the wit of man." Hamilton paused and said, "purge it of its corruption and give to its popular branch equality of representation and it would become an impracticable government; as it stands at present, with all its supposed defects, it is the most perfect government which ever existed." And this was assuredly the exact line which separated the political creed of these two gentlemen. The one was for hereditary branches, and an honest elective one; the other for an hereditary king with a House of Lords and Commons corrupted to his will, and standing between him and the people. Hamilton has indeed a singular character. Of acute understanding, disinterested, honest, and honorable in all private transactions, amiable in society, and duly valuing virtue in private life, yet so bewitched and perverted by the British example as to be under thorough conviction that corruption was essential to the government of a nation.[2]

To James Madison. 1783.

Re. John Adams

His vanity is a lineament in his character which has entirely escaped me. His want of taste I had observed. Notwithstanding all this, he has a sound head on substantial points, and I think he has integrity. I am glad, therefore, he is of the commission for negotiating peace and expect he will be useful in it. His dislike of all parties, and all men, by balancing his prejudices, may give them some fair play to his reason as would a general benevolence of temper.[3]

To Washington. 1791.   *Re. John Adams.*

I am afraid the indiscretion of a printer has committed me with my friend Mr. Adams, for whom as one of the most honest and disinterested men alive I have a cordial esteem, increased by long habits of concurrence in opinion in the days of his Republicanism; and ever since his apostasy to hereditary monarchy and nobility, though we differ, we differ as friends should do.[4]

To Samuel Adams. 1800.   *Re. Samuel Adams.*

A letter from you, my respectable friend, after three and twenty years of separation, has given me a pleasure I cannot express. It recalls to my mind the anxious days we then passed in struggling for mankind. Your principles have been tested in the crucible of time and have come out pure. You have proved that it was monarchy, and not merely British monarchy, you opposed. A government by representation, elected by the people at short periods, was our object; and our maxim at that day was "where annual election ends, tyranny begins," nor have our departures from it been sanctioned by the happiness of their effect.[5]

To John Adams. Philadelphia, July 17, 1791.

Dear Sir—I have a dozen times taken up my pen to write to you and as often laid it down again, suspended between opposing considerations. I determine however to write from a conviction that truth, between candid minds, can never do harm. The first of Paine's pamphlets on the Rights of Man, which came to hand here, belonged to Mr. Beckley. He lent it to Mr. Madison who lent it to me; and while I was reading it Mr. Beckley called on me for it, and as I had not finished it, he desired me, as soon as I should have done so, to send it to Mr. Jonathan B. Smith, whose brother meant to reprint it. I finished reading it, and as I had no acquaintance with Mr. Jonathan B. Smith, propriety required that I should explain to him why I, a stranger to him, sent him the pamphlet. I accordingly wrote a note of compliment informing him that I did it at the desire of Mr. Beckley, and, to take off a little of the dryness of the note, I added that I was glad it was to be reprinted here and that something was to be publicly said against the political heresies which had sprung up among us, etc. I thought so little of this note that I did not even keep a copy of it: nor ever heard a tittle more of it till, the week following, I was thunderstruck with seeing it come out at the head of the pamphlet. I hoped however it would not attract notice. But I found on my return from a journey of a month that a writer came forward under the signature of Publicola, attacking not only the author and principles of the pamphlet, but myself as its sponsor, by name. Soon after came hosts of other writers defending the pamphlet and attacking you by name as the writer of Publicola. Thus were our names thrown on the public stage as public antagonists. That you and I differ in our ideas of the best form of government is well known to us both: but we have differed as friends should do, respecting the purity of each other's motives, and confining our difference of opinion to private conversation. And I can declare with truth in the presence of the Almighty that nothing was further from my intention or expectation than to have either my own or your name brought before the public on this occasion. The friendship and confidence which has so long existed between us required this explanation from me, and I know you too well to fear any misconstruction of the motives of it. Some people here who would wish me to be, or to be thought, guilty of improprieties, have suggested that I was Agricola, that I was Brutus etc., etc. I never did in my life, either by myself or by any other, have a sentence of mine inserted in a newspaper without putting my name to it; and I believe I never shall.[6]

To Thomas Cooper. Washington, July 9, 1807.

Dear Sir—Your favor of June 23 is received. I had not beforehand learned that a life of Dr. Priestley had been published, or I should certainly have procured it; for no man living had a more affectionate respect for him. In religion, in politics, in physics, no man has rendered more service.

I had always expected that when the republicans should have put down all things under their feet, they would schismatize among themselves. I always expected, too, that whatever names the parties might bear, the real division would be into moderate and ardent republicanism. In this division there is no great evil,—not even if the minority obtain the ascendency by the accession of federal votes to their candidate; because this gives us one shade only, instead of another, of republicanism. It is to be considered as apostasy only when they purchase the votes of federalists, with a participation in honor and power. The gross insult lately received from the English has forced the latter into a momentary coalition with the mass of republicans; but the moment we begin to act in the very line they have joined in approving, all will be wrong, and every act the reverse of what it should have been. Still, it is better to admit their coalescence, and leave to themselves their short-lived existence.[7]

To Gideon Granger. Monticello, March 9, 1814.

Here I do not recollect the particulars; but I have a general recollection that Colonel Burr's conduct had already, at that date rendered his designs suspicious; that being for that reason laid aside by his constituents as Vice President, and aiming to become the Governor of New York, it was thought advisable that the persons of influence in that State should be put on their guard; and Mr. Clinton being eminent, no one was more likely to receive intimations from us, nor any one more likely to be confided in for their communication than yourself. I have no doubt therefore of the fact, and the less because in your letter to me of October 9, 1806, you remind me of it.

About the same period, that is, in the winter of 1803-4,

another train of facts took place which, although not specifically stated in your letter, I think it but justice to yourself that I should state. I mean the intrigues which were in agitation, and at the bottom of which we believed Colonel Burr to be; to form a coalition of the five eastern States, with New York and New Jersey, under the new appellation of the seven eastern States; either to overawe the Union by the combination of their power and their will, or by threats of separating themselves from it. Your intimacy with some of those in the secret gave you opportunities of searching into their proceedings, of which you made me daily and confidential reports. This intimacy to which I had such useful recourse, at the time, rendered you an object of suspicion with many as being yourself a partisan of Colonel Burr, and engaged in the very combination which you were faithfully employed in defeating. I never failed to justify you to all those who brought their suspicions to me, and to assure them of my knowledge of your fidelity. Many were the individuals, then members of the legislature, who received these assurances from me, and whose apprehensions were thereby quieted. This first project of Colonel Burr having vanished in smoke, he directed to the western country those views which are the subject of your next article.

"That in 1806, I communicated by the first mail after I had got knowledge of the fact, the supposed plans of Burr in his western expedition; upon which communication your council was first called together to take measures in relation to that subject." Not exactly on that single communication; on the 15th and 18th of September, I had received letters from Colonel George Morgan, and from a

Mr. Nicholson of New York, suggesting in a general way the maneuvers of Colonel Burr. Similar information came to the Secretary of State from a Mr. Williams of New York. The indications, however, were so vague that I only desired their increased attention to the subject, and further communications of what they should discover. Your letter of October 16, conveying the communications of General Eaton to yourself and to Mr. Ely gave a specific view of the objects of this new conspiracy, and corroborating our previous information, I called the Cabinet together, on the 22nd of October, when specific measures were adopted for meeting the dangers threatened in the various points in which they might occur. I say your letter of October 16 gave this information, because its date, with the circumstance of its being no longer on my files, induces me to infer it was that particular letter, which having been transferred to the bundle of the documents of that conspiracy, delivered to the Attorney General, is no longer in my possession.[s]

To The Marquis de Lafayette.

Monticello, February 14, 1815.

With us the affairs of war have taken the most favorable turn which was to be expected. Our thirty years of peace had taken off, or superannuated, all our revolutionary officers of experience and grade; and our first draught in the lottery of untried characters had been most unfortunate. The delivery of the fort and army of Detroit by the traitor Hull; the disgrace at Queenstown, under Van Rensellaer; the massacre at Frenchtown under Winchester; and surrender of Boerstler in an open field to one third of his own numbers, were the inauspicious beginnings of the first year of our warfare. The second witnessed but the single miscarriage occasioned by the disagreement of Wilkinson and Hampton, mentioned in my letter to you of November the 30th, 1813, while it gave us the capture of York by Dearborne and Pike; the capture of Fort George by Dearborne also; the capture of Proctor's army on the Thames by Harrison, Shelby and Johnson, and that of the whole British fleet on Lake Erie by Perry. The third year has been a continued series of victories, to-wit: of Brown and Scott at Chippewa, of the same at Niagara; of Gaines over Drummond at Fort Erie; that of Brown over Drummond at the same place; the capture of another fleet on Lake Champlain by M'Donough; the entire defeat of their army under Prevost, on the same day, by M'Comb, and recently their defeats at New Orleans by Jackson, Coffee and Carroll, with the loss of four thousand men out of nine thousand and six hundred, with their two Generals, Packingham and Gibbs killed, and a third, Keane, wounded, mortally, as is said.

This series of successes has been tarnished only by the conflagration at Washington, a *coup de main* differing from that at Richmond, which you remember, in the revolutionary war, in the circumstance only, that we had, in that case, but forty-eight hours' notice that an enemy had arrived within our capes; whereas, at Washington, there was abundant previous notice. The force designated by the President was double of what was necessary; but failed, as is the general opinion, through the insubordination of Armstrong, who would never believe the attack intended until it was actually made, and the sluggishness of Winder

before the occasion, and his indecision during it. Still, in
the end, the transaction has helped rather than hurt us, by
arousing the general indignation of our country, and by
marking to the world of Europe the Vandalism and brutal
character of the English government. It has merely served
to immortalize their infamy. And add further, that through
the whole period of the war, we have beaten them singlehanded at sea, and so thoroughly established our superi-
ority over them with equal force, that they retire from that
kind of contest, and never suffer their frigates to cruise
singly. The Endymion would never have engaged the frigate President, but knowing herself backed by three frigates
and a razee, who, though somewhat slower sailers, would
get up before she could be taken. The disclosure to the
world of the fatal secret that they can be beaten at sea with
an equal force, the evidence furnished by the military
operations of the last year that experience is rearing us
officers who, when our means shall be fully under way,
will plant our standard on the walls of Quebec and Hali-
fax, their recent and signal disaster at New Orleans, and
the evaporation of their hopes from the Hartford convention, will probably raise a clamor in the British nation,
which will force their ministry into peace. I say *force* them,
because, willingly, they would never be at peace. The British ministers find in a state of war rather than of peace,
by riding the various contractors, and receiving *douceurs*
on the vast expenditures of the war supplies, that they
recruit their broken fortunes, or make new ones, and
therefore will not make peace as long as by any delusions
they can keep the temper of the nation up to the war point.
They found some hopes on the state of our finances. It is

true that the excess of our banking institutions, and their present discredit, have shut us out from the best source of credit we could ever command with certainty. But the foundations of credit still remain to us, and need but skill which experience will soon produce, to marshal them into an order which may carry us through any length of war. But they have hoped more in their Hartford convention. Their fears of republican France being now done away, they are directed to republican America, and they are playing the same game for disorganization here, which they played in your country. The Marats, the Dantons and Robespierres of Massachusetts are in the same pay, under the same orders, and making the same efforts to anarchise us, that their prototypes in France did there.

I do not say that all who met at Hartford were under the same motives of money, nor were those of France. Some of them are Outs, and wish to be Ins; some the mere dupes of the agitators, or of their own party passions, while the Maratists alone are in the real secret; but they have very different materials to work on. The yeomanry of the United States are not the *canaille* of Paris. We might safely give them leave to go through the United States recruiting their ranks, and I am satisfied they could not raise one single regiment (gambling merchants and silk-stocking clerks excepted) who would support them in any effort to separate from the Union. The cement of this Union is in the heart-blood of every American. I do not believe there is on earth a government established on so immovable a basis. Let them, in any State, even in Massachusetts itself, raise the standard of separation, and its citizens will rise in mass, and do justice themselves on their own incendiaries. If they could have induced the government to some effort of suppression, or even to enter into discussion with them, it would have given them some importance, have brought them into some notice. But they have not been able to make themselves even a subject of conversation, either of public or private societies. A silent contempt has been the sole notice they excite; consoled, indeed, some of them, by the *palpable* favors of Philip. Have then no fears for us, my friend. The grounds of these exist only in English newspapers, endited or endowed by the Castlereaghs or the Cannings, or some other such models of pure and uncorrupted virtue. Their military heroes, by land and sea, may sink our oyster boats, rob our hen roosts, burn our negro huts, and run off. But a campaign or two more will relieve them from further trouble or expense in defending their American possessions.

You once gave me a copy of the journal of your campaign in Virginia, in 1781, which I must have lent to some one of the undertakers to write the history of the revolutionary war, and forgot to reclaim. I conclude this, because it is no longer among my papers, which I have very diligently searched for it, but in vain. An author of real ability is now writing that part of the history of Virginia. He does it in my neighborhood, and I lay open to him all my papers. But I possess none, nor has he any, which can enable him to do justice to your faithful and able services in that campaign. If you could be so good as to send me another copy, by the very first vessel bound to any port in the United States, it might be here in time; for although he expects to begin to print within a month or two, yet you know the delays of these undertakings. At any rate it might be got in as a supplement. The old Count Rochambeau gave me also his *memoire* of the operations at York, which is gone in the same way, and I have no means of applying to his family for it. Perhaps you could render them as well as us, the service of procuring another copy . . .

This letter will be handed you by Mr. Tinknor, a young gentleman of Boston, of great erudition, indefatigable industry, and preparation for a life of distinction in his own country. He passed a few days with me here, brought high recommendations from Mr. Adams and others, and appeared in every respect to merit them. He is well worthy of those attentions which you so kindly bestow on our countrymen, and for those he may receive I shall join him in acknowledging personal obligations.

I salute you with assurances of my constant and affectionate friendship and respect.

P.S. February 26th. My letter had not yet been sealed, when I received news of our peace. I am glad of it, and especially that we closed our war with the eclat of the action at New Orleans. But I consider it as an armistice only, because no security is provided against the impressment of our seamen. While this is unsettled we are in hostility of mind with England, although actual deeds of arms may be suspended by a truce. If she thinks the exercise of this outrage is worth eternal war, eternal war it must· be, or extermination of the one or the other party. The first act of impressment she commits on an American, will be answered by reprisal, or by a declaration of war here; and the interval must be merely a state of preparation for it.

In this we have much to do, in further fortifying our seaport towns, providing military stores, classing and disciplining our militia, arranging our financial system, and above all pushing our domestic manufactures, which have taken such root as never again can be shaken. Once more, God bless you.[9]

To John Adams. Monticello, August 10, 1815.

On the subject of the history of the American Revolution, you ask who shall write it? Who can Write it? And who will ever be able to write it? Nobody; except merely its external facts; all its councils, designs and discussions having been conducted by Congress with closed doors, and no members, as far as I know, having even made notes of them. These, which are the life and soul of history, must be forever unknown. Botta, as you observe, has put his own speculations and reasonings into the mouths of persons whom he names, but who, you and I know, never made such speeches. In this he has followed the example of the ancients, who made their great men deliver long speeches, all of them in the same style, and in that of the author himself. The work is nevertheless a good one, more judicious, more chaste, more classical, and more true than the party diatribe of Marshall. Its greatest fault is in having taken too much from him. I possessed the work, and often recurred to considerable portions of it, although I never read it through. But a very judicious and well-informed neighbor of mine went through it with great attention, and spoke very highly of it. I have said that no member of the old Congress, as far as I knew, made notes of the discussion. I did not know of the speeches you mention of Dickinson and Witherspoon. But on the questions of Independence, and on the two articles of Confederation respecting taxes and votings, I took minutes of the heads of the arguments. On the first, I threw all into one-mass, without ascribing to the speakers their respective arguments; pretty much in the manner of Hume's summary digests of the reasonings of parliament for and against a measure. On the last, I stated the heads of the arguments used by each speaker. But the whole of my notes on the question of Independence does not occupy more than five pages, such as of this letter; and on the other questions, two such sheets. They have never been communicated to any one. Do you know that there exists in manuscript the ablest work of this kind ever yet executed, of the debates of the constitutional convention of Philadelphia in 1788? The whole of everything said and done there was taken down by Mr. Madison, with a labor and exactness beyond comprehension.[10]

To Benjamin Waterhouse. Monticello, October 13, 1815.

Dear Sir—I was highly gratified with the receipt of your letter of Sept. 1 by Genl. and Mrs. Dearborne; and by the evidence it furnished me of your bearing up with firmness and perseverance against the persecutions of your enemies, religious, political and professional. These last I suppose have not yet forgiven you the introduction of vaccination and annihilation of the great variolous field of profit to them: and none of them pardon the proof you have established that the condition of man may be meliorated, if not *infinitely,* as enthusiasm alone pretends, yet *indefinitely,* as bigots alone can doubt. In lieu of these enmities you have the blessings of all the friends of human happiness, for this great peril from which they are rescued . . .

These reverend leaders of the Hartford nation it seems then are now falling together about religion, of which they have not one real principle in their hearts. Like bawds, religion becomes to them a refuge from the despair of their loathsome vices. They seek in it only an oblivion of the disgrace with which they have loaded themselves, in their political ravings, and of their mortification at the ridiculous issue of their Hartford convention. No event, more than this, has shown the placid character of our constitution. Under any other their treasons would have been punished by the halter. We let them live as laughing stocks for the world, and punish them by the torment of eternal contempt. The emigrations you mention from the Eastern states are what I have long counted on. The religious and political tyranny of those in power with you, cannot fail to drive the oppressed to milder associations of men, where freedom of mind is allowed in fact as well as in pretence.[11]

Wars and rumors of wars, our payment of an annual tribute to Algeria, "So many revolutions going on in different countries at the same time, such combinations of tyranny and military preparations and movements to suppress them" sound a modern note in this group of letters on Wars and Treaties.

Foreign Wars and Treaties

To William Carmichael. Paris, June 3, 1788.

Dear Sir—With respect to the *isthmus of Panama* I am assured by *Burgoyne* (who would not choose to be named however) that a *survey* was made, that a *canal* appeared very practicable, and that the idea was suppressed for *political reasons* altogether. He has seen and minutely examined the *report*. This *report* is to me a vast desideratum for reason *political and philosophical*. I cannot help suspecting the Spanish squadron to be gone to S. America, and that some disturbances have been excited there by the British. The court of Madrid may suppose we would not see this with an unwilling eye. This may be true as to the uninformed part of our people: but those who look into futurity farther than the present moment or age, and who combine well what is, with what is to be, must see that our interests, well understood, and our wishes are that Spain shall (not forever, but) very long retain her possessions in that quarter. And that her views and ours must, in a good degree, and for a long time, concur. It is said in our gazettes that the Spaniards have sunk one of our boats on the Mississippi, and that our people retaliated on one of theirs. But my letters not mentioning this fact have made me hope it is not true, in which hope your letter confirms me. There are now 100,000 inhabitants at

Kentucky. They have accepted the offer of independence on the terms proposed by Virginia and they have decided that their independent government shall begin on the 1st. day of the next year. In the meantime they claim admittance into Congress. Georgia has ceded her western territory to the U. S. to take place with the commencement of the new federal government.[17]

To James Monroe. New York, July 11, 1790.

Dear Sir—I wrote you last on the 20th of June. The bill for removing the federal government to Philadelphia for 10 years and then to Georgetown has at length passed both houses. The offices are to be removed before the first of December. I presume it will be done during the President's trip to Virginia about the 1st of September and October. I hope to set out for Virgina about the 1st of September and to pass three or four weeks at Monticello. Congress will now probably proceed in better humour to funding the public debt. This measure will secure to us the credit we now hold at Amsterdam, where our European paper is above par, which is the case of no other nation. Our business is to have great credit and to use it little. Whatever enables us to go to war, secures our peace. At present it is essential to let Spain and England see that we are in a condition for war, for a number of collateral circumstances now render it probable that they will be in that condition. Our object is to feed and theirs to fight. If we are not forced by England, we shall have a gainful time of it.—A vessel from Gibraltar of the 10th of June tells us O'Hara was busily fortifying and providing there, and that the English Consuls in the Spanish ports on the

Mediterranean had received orders to dispatch all their vessels from those ports immediately. The Captain saw 15 Spanish ships of war going to Cadiz. It is said that Arnold is at Detroit reviewing the militia there. Other symptoms indicate a general design on all Louisiana and the two Floridas. What a tremendous position would success in these objects place us in! Embraced from the St. Croix to the St. Mary's on one side by their possessions, on the other side by their fleet, we need not hesitate to say that they would soon find means to unite to them all the territory covered by the ramifications of the Mississippi. Mrs. Monroe's friends were well three or four days ago. We are all disappointed at her not coming here.[18]

Report on a Convention with Spain, March 22, 1792.

Treason. This, when real, merits the highest punishment. But most codes extend their definitions of treason to acts not really against one's country. They do not distinguish between acts against the *government,* and acts *against the Oppressions of the Government.* The latter are virtues: yet have furnished more victims to the Executioner than the former. Because real Treasons are rare: Oppressions frequent. The unsuccessful struggles against tyranny have been the chief Martyrs of Treason Laws in all countries . . . We should not wish then to give up to the Executioner the Patriot who fails, and flees to us. Treasons then, taking the *simulated* with the *real,* are sufficiently punished by Exile.[1]

To James Madison. Philadelphia, May 31, 1798.

The bill from the Senate for capturing French armed

vessels found hovering on our coast, was passed in two days by the lower House, without a single alteration; and the Ganges, a twenty-gun sloop, fell down the river instantly to go on a cruise. She has since been ordered to New York, to convoy a vessel from that to this port. The alien-bill will be ready today, probably, for its third reading in the Senate. It has been considerably mollified, particularly by a proviso saving the rights of treaties. Still, it is a most detestable thing. I was glad, in yesterday's discussion, to hear it admitted on all hands, that laws of the United States, subsequent to a treaty, control its operation, and that the legislature is the only power which can control a treaty. Both points are sound beyond doubt.[2]

To Thomas Lomax. Monticello, March 12, 1799.

I sincerely join you in abjuring all political connection with every foreign power; and though I cordially wish well to the progress of liberty in all nations, and would forever give it the weight of our countenance, yet they are not to be touched without contamination from their other bad principles. Commerce with all nations, alliance with none, should be our motto.[3]

To Wilson Cary Nicholas. Washington, June 11, 1801.

Dear Sir—A moment of leisure permits me to think of my friends. You will have seen an alarm in the newspapers on the subject of the Tripolitans and Algerines. The former about May a twelvemonth demanded a sum of money for *keeping* the peace, pretending that the sum paid as the price of the treaty was only for *making* peace. This demand was reiterated through the last year, but a promise made to Cathcart by the bey, that he would not permit any hostility until an answer should be actually received from the President. However, I think there is reason to apprehend he sent his cruisers out against us in March. Great notice had been given our vessels in the Mediterranean, so that they might have come off at leisure if they would. In March, finding we might with propriety call in our cruiser from the W. Indies, this was done; and as 2 were to be kept armed, it was thought best by Stoddert and Genl. Smith that we should send three with a tender into the Mediterranean to protect our commerce against Tripoli. But as this might lead to war, I wished to have the approbation of the new administration. In the meantime the squadron was to be prepared and to rendezvous at Norfolk ready to receive our orders. It was the 15th of May before Mr. Gallatin's arrival enabled us to decide definitely. It was then decided unanimously; but it was not until the 25th of May that the Philadelphia reached the rendezvous. On the 1st of June they sailed. With respect to Algiers they are in extreme ill humor. We find 3 years arrears of tribute due to them. This you know has not proceeded from any want of the treasury. Our tribute to them is nominally 20,000 D. to be delivered in stores, but so stated that they cost us 80,000 D. A negotiation had been set on foot by our predecessors to commute the stores for 30,000 D. cash. It would be an excellent bargain, but we know nothing of the result. We have however sent them 30,000 D. by our frigates as one year's tribute, and have a vessel ready to sail with the stores for another year. Letters from the Mediterranean to the last of April give us no reason to think they will commit hostilities. The loose articles in the newspapers have probably arisen by confounding them with the Tripolitans. We have taken these steps towards supplying the deficiencies of our predecessors merely in obedience to the law; being convinced it is money thrown away, and that there is no end to the demand of these powers, nor any security in their promises. The real alternative before us is whether to abandon the Mediterranean or to keep up a cruise in it, perhaps in rotation with other powers who would join us as soon as there is peace. But this Congress must decide.[4]

To James Bowdoin, Minister to Spain.

Washington, April 27, 1805.

Dear Sir—Your favor of March 25 has been duly received. I regret that the state of your health renders a visit to this place unadvisable. Besides the gratification we should have felt from personal considerations, the perusal of the correspondences, for some time back, with the governments of Europe most interesting to us, by putting you in possession of the actual state of things between us, would have enabled you to act under all emergencies with that satisfaction to yourself which is derived from a full knowledge of the ground. But I presume you will find this supplied, as to the government to which you go, by the papers of the office at Madrid. Our relations with that nation are vitally interesting. That they should be of a peaceable and friendly character has been our most earnest desire. Had Spain met us with the same dispositions, our idea was that her existence in this hemisphere and ours, should have rested on the same bottom; should have swam or sunk together. We want nothing of hers, and we want no other nation to possess what is hers. But she has met our advances with jealousy, secret malice and ill-faith. Our patience under this unworthy return of disposition is now on its last trial. And the issue of what is now depending between us will decide whether our relations with her are to be sincerely friendly, or permanently hostile. I still wish and would cherish the former, but have ceased to expect it.[5]

To James Madison, Secretary of State.
Monticello, August 27, 1805.

. . . Considering the character of Bonaparte, I think it material at once to let him see that we are not one of the powers who will receive his orders.

I think you have misconceived the nature of the treaty I thought we should propose to England. I have no idea of committing ourselves immediately or independently of our further will to the war. The treaty should be provisional only, to come into force on the event of our being engaged in war with either France or Spain during the present war in Europe. In that event we should make common cause, and England should stipulate not to make peace without our obtaining the objects for which we go to war to wit, the acknowledgment by Spain of the rightful boundaries of Louisiana (which we should reduce to our minimum by a secret article) and 2, indemnification for spoliations, for which purpose we should be allowed to make reprisal on the Floridas and *retain them* as an indemnification. Our co-operation in the war (if we should actually enter into it) would be a sufficient consideration for Great Britain to engage for its object; and it being generally known to France and Spain that we had entered into treaty with England, would probably ensure us a peaceable and immediate settlement of both points. But another motive much more powerful would indubitably induce England to go much further. Whatever ill-humor may at times have been expressed against us by individuals of that country, the first wish of every Englishman's heart is to see us once more fighting by their sides against France; nor could the king and his ministers do an act so popular as to enter into an alliance with us. The nation would not weigh the consideration by grains and scruples. They would consider it as the price and pledge of an indissoluble course of friendship. I think it possible that for such a provisional treaty they would give us their general guarantee of Louisiana and the Floridas. At any rate we might try them. A failure would not make our situation worse. If such a one could be obtained we might await our own convenience for calling up the *casus foederis*. I think it important that England should receive an overture as early as possible, as it might prevent her listening to terms of peace. If I recollect rightly, we instructed Monroe, when he went to Paris, to settle the deposit; if he failed in that object to propose a treaty to England immediately. We could not be more engaged to secure the deposit then, than we are the country now, after paying 15 millions for it. I do expect, therefore, that considering the present state of things as analogous to that, and virtually within his instructions, he will very likely make the proposition to England. I write my thoughts freely, wishing the same from the other gentlemen, that seeing and considering the ground of each other's opinions we may come as soon as possible to a result. I propose to be in Washington on the 2nd of October. By that time I hope we shall be ripe for some conclusion.[6]

To Caesar A. Rodney. Monticello, February 10, 1810.

My Dear Sir—I have to thank you for your favor of the 31st ultimo, which is just now received. It has been peculiarly unfortunate for us, personally, that the portion in the history of mankind, at which we were called to take a share in the direction of their affairs, was such an one as history has never before presented. At any other period, the even-handed justice we have observed towards all nations, the efforts we have made to merit their esteem by every act which candor or liberality could exercise, would have preserved our peace, and secured the unqualified confidence of all other nations in our faith and probity. But the hurricane which is now blasting the world, physical and moral, has prostrated all the mounds of reason as well as right. All those calculations which, at any other period, would have been deemed honorable, of the existence of a moral sense in man, individually or associated . . . have been a matter of reproach on us, as evidences of imbecility. As if it could be a folly for an honest man to suppose that others could be honest also, when it is their interest to be so. And when is this state of things to end? The death of Bonaparte would, to be sure, remove the first and chiefest apostle of the desolation of men and morals, and might withdraw the scourge of the land. But what is to restore order and safety on the ocean? The death of George III? Not at all. He is only stupid; and his ministers, however weak and profligate in morals, are ephemeral. But his nation is permanent, and it is that which is the tyrant of the ocean. The principal that force is right, is become the principle of the nation itself. They would not permit an honest minister, were accident to bring such an one into power, to relax their system of lawless piracy.[7]

To William Wirt. Monticello, May 3, 1811.

War against Bedlam would be just as rational as against Europe in its present condition of total demoralization. When peace becomes more losing than war, we may prefer the latter on principles of pecuniary calculation. But for us to attempt, by war, to reform all Europe, and bring them back to principles of morality and a respect for the equal rights of nations, would show us to be only maniacs of another character. We should, indeed, have the merit of good intentions as well as of the folly of the hero of La Mancha.[8]

To James Madison. 1814.

We cannot too distinctly detach ourselves from the European system, which is essentially belligerent, nor too sedulously cultivate an American system, which is essentially pacific. But if we go into commercial treaties at all, they should be with all, at the same time, with whom we have important commercial relations. France, Spain, Portugal, Holland, Denmark, Sweden, Russia, all should proceed *pari passu*. Our ministers marching in phalanx on the same line, and intercommunicating freely, each will be supported by the weight of the whole mass, and the facility with which the other nations will agree to equal terms of intercourse, will discountenance the selfish higglings of

England, or justify our rejection of them. . . . leaving everything to the usages and courtesies of civilized nations.[9]

To the Marquis De LaFayette.

Monticello, February 14, 1815.

My Dear Friend—Your letter of August the 14th has been received and read again, and again, with extraordinary pleasure. It is the first glimpse which has been furnished me of the interior workings of the late unexpected but fortunate revolution of your country. The newspapers told us only that the great beast was fallen; but what part in this the patriots acted, and what the egotists, whether the former slept while the latter were awake to their own interests only, the hireling scribblers of the English press said little and knew less. I see now the mortifying alternative under which the patriot there is placed, of being either silent, or disgraced by an association in opposition with the remains of Bonapartism. A full measure of liberty is not now perhaps to be expected by your nation, nor am I confident they are prepared to preserve it. More than a generation will be requisite, under the administration of reasonable laws favoring the progress of knowledge in the general mass of the people, and their habituation to an independent security of person and property, before they will be capable of estimating the value of freedom, and the necessity of a sacred adherence to the principles on which it rests for preservation. Instead of that liberty which takes root and growth in the progress of reason, if recovered by mere force or accident, it becomes, with an unprepared people, a tyranny still, of the many, the few, or the one. Possibly you may remember, at the date of the *jue de*

paume, how earnestly I urged yourself and the patriots of
my acquaintance, to enter then into a compact with the
king, securing freedom of religion, freedom of the press,
trial by jury, *habeas corpus,* and a national legislature, all
of which it was known he would then yield, to go home,
and let these work on the amelioration of the condition of
the people, until they should have rendered them capable
of more, when occasions would not fail to arise for communicating to them more. This was as much as I then
thought them able to bear, soberly and usefully for themselves. You thought otherwise, and that the dose might
still be larger. And I found you were right; for subsequent
events proved they were equal to the constitution of 1791.
Unfortunately, some of the most honest and enlightened of
our patriotic friends, (but closet politicians merely, un-
practised in the knowledge of man,) thought more could
still be obtained and borne. They did not weigh the hazards of a transition from one form of government to another, the value of what they had already rescued from
those hazards, and might hold in security if they pleased,
nor the imprudence of giving up the certainty of such a
degree of liberty, under a limited monarch, for the uncertainty of a little more under the form of a republic.
You differed from them. You were for stopping there, and
for securing the constitution which the National Assembly
had obtained. Here, too, you were right; and from this
fatal error of the republicans, from their separation from
yourself and the constitutionalists, in their councils, flowed
all subsequent sufferings and crimes of the French nation.
The hazards of a second change fell upon them by the
way. The foreigner gained time to anarchise by gold the

government he could not overthrow by arms, to crush in their own councils the genuine republicans, by the fraternal embraces of exaggerated and hired pretenders, and to turn the machine of Jacobinism from the change to the destruction of order; and, in the end, the limited monarchy they had secured was exchanged for the unprincipled and bloody tyranny of Robespierre, and the equally unprincipled and maniac tyranny of Bonaparte. You are now rid of him, and I sincerely wish you may continue so. But this may depend on the wisdom and moderation of the restored dynasty. It is for them now to read a lesson in the fatal errors of the republicans; to be contented with a certain portion of power, secured by formal compact with the nation, rather than, grasping at more, hazard all upon uncertainty, and risk meeting the fate of their predecessor, or a renewal of their own exile. We are just informed, too, of an example which merits, if true, their most profound contemplation. The gazettes say that Ferdinand of Spain is dethroned, and his father re-established on the basis of their new constitution. This order of magistrates must, therefore, see, that although the attempts at reformation have not succeeded in their whole length, and some secession from the ultimate point has taken place, yet that men have by no means fallen back to their former passiveness, but on the contrary, that a sense of their rights, and a restlessness to obtain them, remain deeply impressed on every mind, and, if not quieted by a reasonable relaxation of power, will break out like a volcano on the first occasion, and overwhelm everything again in its way. I always thought the present king an honest and moderate man; and having no issue, he is under a motive the less

for yielding to personal considerations. I cannot, therefore, but hope, that the patriots in and out of your legislature, acting in phalanx, but temperately and wisely, press-
ing unremittingly the principles omitted in the late capitulation of the king, and watching the occasions which the
course of events will create, may get those principles en-
grafted into it, and sanctioned by the solemnity of a national act.[10]

To John Adams. Monticello, August 10, 1815.

. . . I presume that our correspondence has been observed at the post offices, and thus has attracted notice.
Would you believe, that a printer has had the effrontery
to propose to me the letting him publish it? These people
think they have a right to everything, however secret or
sacred. I had not heard of the Boston pamphlet with
Priestley's letters and mine.

At length Bonaparte has got on the right side of a question. From the time of his entering the legislative hall to
his retreat to Elba, no man has execrated him more than
myself. I will not except even the members of the Essex
Junto; although for very different reasons; I, because he
was warring against the liberty of his own country, and
independence of others; they, because he was the enemy of
England, the Pope, and the Inquisition. But at length, and
as far as we can judge, he seems to have become the choice
of his nation. At least, he is defending the cause of his
nation, and that of all mankind, the rights of every people
to independence and self-government. He and the allies
have now changed sides. They are parcelling out among
themselves Poland, Belgium, Saxony, Italy; dictating a rul-

er and government to France, and looking askance at our republic, the splendid libel on their governments, and he is fighting for the principles of national independence, of which his whole life hitherto has been a continued violation. He has promised a free government to his own country, and to respect the rights of others; and although his former conduct inspires little confidence in his promises, yet we had better take the chance of his word for doing right, than the certainty of the wrong which his adversaries are doing and avowing. If they succeed, ours is only the boon of the Cyclops to Ulysses, of being the last devoured.[11]

To Benjamin Austin. Monticello. January 9, 1816.

Your opinions on the events which have taken place in France, are entirely just, so far as these events are yet developed. But they have not reached their ultimate termination. There is still an awful void between the present and what is to be the last chapter of that history; and I fear it is to be filled with abominations as frightful as those which have already disgraced it. That nation is too high-minded, has too much innate force, intelligence and elasticity, to remain under its present compression. Samson will arise in his strength, as of old, and as of old will burst asunder the withes and the cords, and the webs of the Philistines. But what are to be the scenes of havoc and horror, and how widely they may spread between the brethren of the same house, our ignorance of the interior feuds and antipathies of the country places beyond our ken. It will end, nevertheless, in a representative government, in a government in which the will of the people will be an effective ingredient. This important element has taken root in the European mind, and will have its growth; their despots, sensible of this, are already offering this modification of their governments, as if of their own accord. Instead of the parricide treason of Bonaparte, in perverting the means confided to him as a republican magistrate, to the subversion ᴏf that republic and erection of a military despotism for himself and his family, had he used it honestly for the establishment and support of a free government in his own country, France would now have been in freedom and rest; and her example operating in a contrary direction, every nation in Europe would have had a government over which the will of the people would have had some control. His atrocious egotism has checked the salutary progress of principle, and deluged it with rivers of blood which are not yet run out. To the vast sum of devastation and of human misery, of which he has been the guilty cause, much is still to be added. But the object is fixed in the eye of nations, and they will press on to its accomplishment and to the general amelioration of the condition of man. What a germ we have planted, and how faithfully should we cherish the parent tree at home![12]

To Benjamin Austin. Monticello, February 9, 1816.

Sir—Your favor of January 25th is just now received. I am in general extremely unwilling to be carried into the newspapers, no matter what the subject; the whole pack of the Essex kennel would open upon me. With respect, however, to so much of my letter of January 9th as relates to manufactures, I have less repugnance, because there is perhaps a degree of duty to avow a change of opinion called for by a change of circumstance, and especially on a point now become peculiarly interesting.

What relates to Bonaparte stands on different ground. You think it will silence the misrepresentations of my enemies as to my opinion of him. No, Sir; it will not silence them. They had no ground either in my words or actions for these misrepresentations before, and cannot have less afterwards; nor will they calumniate less. There is, however, a consideration respecting our own friends, which may merit attention. I have grieved to see even good republicans so infatuated as to this man, as to consider his downfall as calamitous to the cause of liberty. In their indignation against England which is just, they seem to consider all *her* enemies as *our* friends, when it is well known there was not a being on earth who bore us so deadly a hatred. In fact, he saw nothing in this world but himself, and looked on the people under him as his cattle, beasts for burden and slaughter. Promises cost him nothing when they could serve his purpose. On his return from Elba, what did he not promise? But those who had credited them a little, soon saw their total insignificance, and, satisfied they could not fall under worse hands, refused every effort after the defeat of Waterloo. Their present sufferings will have a term; his iron despotism would have had none. France has now a family of fools at its head, from whom, whenever it can shake off its foreign riders, it will extort a free constitution, or dismount them and establish some other on the solid basis of national right. To whine after this exorcised demon is a disgrace to republicans, and must have arisen either from want of reflection, or the indulgence of passion against principle. If anything

I have said could lead them to take correcter views, to rally to the polar principles of genuine republicanism, I could consent that that part of my letter also should go into a newspaper. This I leave to yourself and such candid friends as you may consult. . . .[13]

To Robert Walsh. Monticello, February 6, 1820.

Dear Sir—Continual ill health for 18 months past had nearly ended the business of letter-writing with me. I cannot however but make an effort to thank you for your vindicia Americana against Gr. Britain. The malevolence and impertinence of her critics and writers really called for the rod, and I rejoiced when I heard it was in hands so able to wield it with strength and correctness. Your work will furnish the 1st volume of every future American history; the Ante-revolutionary part especially. The latter part will silence the libellists of the day, who finding refutation impossible, and that men in glass houses should not provoke a war of stones, will be glad of a truce, to hush and be done with it. I wish that, being placed on the vantage ground by these researches and expositions of facts, our own citizens and our antagonists would now bury the hatchet and join in a mutual amnesty. No two nations on earth can be so helpful to each other as friends, nor hurtful as enemies. And, in spite of their insolence I have ever wished for an honorable and cordial amity with them as a nation. I think the looking glass you have held up to them will now so completely humble their pride as to dispose them also to wish and court it.[14]

To Albert Gallatin. Monticello. December 26, 1820.

Looking from our quarter of the world over the horizon

of yours, we imagine we see storms gathering which may again desolate the face of that country. So many revolutions going on in different countries at the same time, such combinations of tyranny and military preparations and movements to suppress them, England and France unsafe from internal conflict, Germany on the first favorable occasion ripe for insurrection, such a state of things, we suppose, must end in war, which needs a kindling spark in one spot only to spread over the whole. Your information can correct these views, which are stated only to inform you of impressions here.[15]

To John Jay. Paris, August 23, 1785.

Our people are decided in the opinion that it is necessary for us to take a share in the occupation of the ocean, and their established habits induce them to require that the sea be kept open to them, and that that line of policy be pursued, which will render the use of that element to them as great as possible. I think it a duty in those entrusted with the administration of their affairs, to conform themselves to the decided choice of their constituents: and that therefore, we should, in every instance, preserve an equality of right to them in the transportation of commodities, in the right of fishing, and in the other uses of the sea.

But what will be the consequence? Frequent wars without a doubt. Their property will be violated on the sea and in foreign ports, their persons will be insulted, imprisoned, etc. for pretended debts, contracts, crimes, contraband, etc., etc. These insults must be resented, even if we had no feelings, yet to prevent their eternal repetition; or, in other words, our commerce on the ocean and in other countries must be paid for by frequent war. The justest dispositions possible in ourselves will not secure us against it. It would be necessary that all other nations were just also. Justice indeed, on our part, will save us from those wars which would have been produced by contrary disposition. But how can we prevent those produced by the wrongs of other nations? By putting ourselves in a condition to punish them. Weakness provokes insult and injury, while a condition to punish, often prevents them. This reasoning leads to the necessity of some naval force; that being the only weapon with which we can reach an enemy. I think it to our interest to punish the first insult: because an insult unpunished is the parent of many others. We are not at this moment in a condition to do it, but we should put ourselves into it, as soon as possible. If a war with England should take place, it seems to me that the first thing necessary, would be a resolution to abandon the carrying trade, because we cannot protect it. Foreign nations must, in that case, be invited to bring us what we want, and to take our productions in their own bottoms. This alone could prevent the loss of those productions to us, and the acquisition of them to our enemy. Our seamen might be employed in depredations on their trade. But how dreadfully shall we suffer on our coasts, if we have no force on the water, former experience has taught us. Indeed, I look forward with horror to the very possible case of war with an European power, and think there is no protection against them, but from the possession of some force on the sea. Our vicinity to their West India possessions and to the fisheries, is a bridle which a small naval force, on our part, would hold in the mouths of the most powerful of these countries. I hope our land office will rid us of our debts, and that our first attention then will be, to the beginning a naval force of some sort. This alone can countenance our people as carriers on the water, and I suppose them to be determined to continue such.[16]

The Constitutional system of checks and balances built into our Federal Government appear to be innocuous enough in mechanical terms. Obviously they are not mechanical, but involve human relationships and frailties. These checks and balances are actually based upon expected conflicts between three great governmental adversaries. During Jefferson's administration, the President and Congress were generally on the best of terms. On the other hand, Jefferson regarded the Supreme Court as a true adversary and this is expressed in most precise terms in a number of letters on the Judiciary.

The Judiciary

To George Wythe. July, 1776.

The dignity and stability of government in all its branches, the morals of the people, and every blessing of society, depend so much upon an upright and skillful administration of justice that the judicial power ought to be distinct from both the legislature and executive, and independent upon both, that so it may be a check upon both, as both should be a check upon that. The judges, therefore, should be men of learning and experience in the laws, of exemplary morals, great patience, calmness and attention; their minds should not be distracted with jarring interests; they should not be dependent upon any body of men. To these ends they should hold estates for life in their offices, or, in other words, their commissions should be during good behavior, and their salaries ascertained and established by law. For misbehavior of judges the grand inquest of the Colony, the House of Representatives, should impeach them before the Governor and Council, when they should have time and opportunity to make their defense; but if convicted, should be removed from their offices and subjected to such other punishment as shall be thought proper.[1]

To M. Claviere. Paris, July 6, 1787.

Sir—The load of business which has accumulated dur-

ing my absence has put it out of my power to answer
sooner the letter & observations with which you were
pleased to honor me. I have perused those observations
with attention, and think them judicious, and well calculated to remedy the evil of public robbers & unsafe high-
roads. But it is a happy truth for us, Sir, that these evils
do not exist, & never did exist in our part of America.
That Sieur de Perponcher has suffered himself to be misled probably by the English papers. I attended the bar of
the Supreme Court of Virginia ten years as a student,
& as a practitioner. There never was during that time a
trial for robbery on the high road, nor do I remember
ever to have heard of one in that or any other of the
states, except in the cities of New York & Philadelphia
immediately after the departure of the British army. Some
deserters from that army infested those cities for a while;
but as I have heard nothing of them for some time past,
I suppose the vigilance of the civil magistrate has suppressed the evils.[2]

To Judge Spencer Roane.

Poplar Forest, September 6, 1819.

The nation (in 1800) declared its will by dismissing
functionaries of one principle and electing those of another
in the two branches, executive and legislative, submitted
to their election. Over the judiciary department the Constitution had deprived them of their control. That, therefore, has continued the reprobated system, and although
new matter has occasionally been incorporated into the
old, yet the leaven of the old mass seems to assimilate to
itself the new, and after twenty years' confirmation of the

federated system by the voice of the nation declared through the medium of election we find the judiciary on every occasion still drawing us into consolidation. In denying the right they usurp of exclusively explaining the Constitution, I go further than you do, if I might understand rightly your quotation from the Federalist of an opinion that "the judiciary is the last resort in relation to the other departments of the government, but not in relation to the rights of the parties to the compact under which the judiciary is derived." If this opinion be sound then indeed is our Constitution a complete *felo de se*. For intending to establish three departments, co-ordinate and independent, that they might check and balance one another, it has given, according to this opinion, to one of them alone, the right to prescribe rules for the government of the others, and to that one too, which is unelected by, and independent of the nation . . . The constitution, on this hypothesis, is a mere thing of wax in the hands of the judiciary, which they may twist and shape into any form they please. It should be remembered, as an axiom of eternal truth in politics, that whatever power in any government is independent, is absolute also; in theory only, at first, while the spirit of the people is up, but in practice, as fast as that relaxes. Independence can be trusted nowhere but with the people in mass. They are inherently independent of all but moral law. My construction of the constitution is very different from what you quote. It is that each department is truly independent of the others, and has an equal right to decide for itself what is the meaning of the constitution in the cases submitted to its action; and especially, where it is to act ultimately and without appeal.

I will explain myself by examples, which, having occurred while I was in office, are better known to me, and the principles which governed them.

A legislature had passed the sedition law. The federal courts had subjected certain individuals to its penalties of fine and imprisonment. On coming into office, I released these individuals by the power of pardon committed to executive discretion, which could never be more properly exercised than where the citizens were suffering without the authority of law, or, which was equivalent, under a law unauthorized by the constitution, and therefore null. In the case of Marbury and Madison, the federal judges declared that commissions, signed and sealed by the President, were valid, although not delivered. I deemed delivery essential to complete a deed, which, as long as it remains in the hands of the party, is as yet no deed, it is in *posse* only, but not in *esse,* and I withheld delivery of the commissions. They cannot issue a mandamus to the President or legislature, or to any of their officers.[3]

To William Charles Jarvis.

Monticello, September 28, 1820.

I thank you, Sir, for the copy of your Republican which you have been so kind as to send me, and I should have acknowledged it sooner but that I am just returned home after a long absence. I have not yet had time to read it seriously, but in looking it over cursorily I see much in it to approve, and shall be glad if it shall lead our youth to the practice of thinking on such subjects and for themselves. That it will have this tendency may be expected, and for that reason I feel an urgency to note what I deem an error in it, the more requiring notice as your opinion is strengthened by that of many others. You seem, in pages 84 and 148, to consider the judges as the ultimate arbiters of all constitutional questions; a very dangerous doctrine indeed, and one which would place us under the despotism of an oligarchy. Our judges are as honest as other men, and not more so. They have, with others, the same passions for party, for power, and the privilege of their corps. Their maxim is *"boni judicis est ampliare jurisdictionem,"* and their power the more dangerous as they are in office for life, and not responsible, as the other functionaries are, to the elective control. The constitution has erected no such single tribunal, knowing that to whatever hands confided, with the corruptions of time and party, its members would become despots. It has more wisely made all the departments co-equal and co-sovereign within themselves. If the legislature fails to pass laws for a census, for paying the judges and other officers of government, for establishing a militia, for naturalization as prescribed by the constitution, or if they fail to meet in congress, the judges cannot issue their mandamus to them; if the President fails to supply the place of a judge, to appoint other civil or military officers, to issue requisite commissions, the judges cannot force him. They can issue their mandamus or distringas to no executive or legislative officer to enforce the fulfillment of their official duties, any more than the president or legislature may issue orders to the judges or their officers. Betrayed by English example, and unaware, as it should seem, of the control of our constitution in this particular, they have at times overstepped their limit by undertaking to command executive officers in the discharge of their executive duties; but the constitution, in keeping three departments distinct and independent, restrains the authority of the judges to judiciary organs, as it does the executive and legislative to executive and legislative organs. The judges certainly have more frequent occasion to act on constitutional questions, because the laws of *meum* and *tuum* and of criminal action, forming the great mass of the system of law, constitute their particular department. When the legislative or executive functionaries act unconstitutionally, they are responsible to the people in their elective capacity. The exemption of the judges from that is quite dangerous enough. I know no safe depository of the ultimate powers of the society but the people themselves; and if we think them not enlightened enough to exercise their control with a wholesome discretion, the remedy is not to take it from them, but to inform their discretion by education. This is the true corrective of abuses of constitutional power. Pardon me, Sir, for this difference of opinion. My personal interest in such questions is entirely extinct, but not my wishes for the longest possible continuance of our government on its pure principles; if the three powers maintain their mutual independence on each other it may last long, but not so if either can assume the authorities of the other. I ask your candid re-consideration of this subject, and am sufficiently sure you will form a candid conclusion.[4]

To Thomas Ritchie. Monticello, December 25, 1820.

The judiciary of the United States is the subtle corps of sappers and miners constantly working underground to undermine the foundations of our confederated fabric. They are construing our Constitution from a co-ordination of a general and special government to a general and supreme one alone. This will lay all things at their feet, and they are too well versed in English law to forget the maxim, *"boni judicis est ampliare jurisdictionem."* We shall see if they are bold enough to take the daring stride their five lawyers have lately taken. If they do, then, with the editor of our book, in his address to the public, I will say, that "against this every man should raise his voice," and more, should uplift his arm. Who wrote this admirable address? Sound, luminous, strong, not a word too much, nor one which can be changed for the worse. That pen should go on, lay bare these wounds of our Constitution, expose the decisions *seriatim,* and arouse, as it is able, the attention of the nation to these bold speculators on its patience. Having found, from experience, that impeachment is an impracticable thing, a mere scare-crow, they consider themselves secure for life; they sculk from responsibility to public opinion, the only remaining hold on them, under a practice first introduced into England by Lord Mansfield, An opinion is huddled up in conclave, perhaps by a majority of one, delivered as if unanimous, and with the silent acquiescence of lazy or timid associates, by a crafty chief judge, who sophisticates the law to his mind, by the turn of his own reasoning. A judiciary law was once reported by the Attorney General to Congress, requiring each judge to deliver his opinion *seriatim* and openly, and then to give it in writing to the clerk to be entered in the record. A judiciary independent of a king or executive alone, is a good thing; but independence of the will of the nation is a solecism, at least in a republican government.[5]

To James Pleasants. Monticello, December 26, 1821.

But you will have a more difficult task in curbing the Judiciary in their enterprises on the constitution. I doubt whether the erection of the Senate into an appellate court on Constitutional questions would be deemed an unexceptionable reliance; because it would enable the judiciary, with the representatives in Senate of one third only of our citizens, and that in a single house, to make *by construction* what they should please of the constitution, and thus bind in a double knot the other two thirds, for I believe that one third of our citizens choose a majority of the Senate, and these too of the smaller states whose interests lead to lessen state influence, and strengthen that of the general government. A better remedy . . . indeed the best I can devise would be to give future commissions to judges for six years (the Senatorial term) with a re-appointment ability by the president with the approbation of *both* houses. That of the H. of Repr. imports a majority of citizens, that of the Senate a majority of states and that of both a majority of the three sovereign departments of the existing government, to wit, of its Executive and legislative branches. If this would not be independence enough, I know not what would be such, short of the total irresponsibility under which we are acting and sinning now. The independence of the judges in England on the King alone is good; but even there they are not independent on the Parliament; being removable on the joint address of both houses, by a vote of a majority of each, but we require a majority of one house and two-thirds of the other, a concurrence which, in practice, has been and ever will be found impossible; for the judiciary perversions of the constitution will forever be protected under the pretext of errors of judgment, which by principle are exempt from punishment. Impeachment therefore is a bugbear which they fear not at all. But they would be under some awe of the canvas of their conduct which would be open to both houses regularly every 6th year. It is a misnomer to call a government republican, in which a branch of the supreme power is independent of the nation. By this change of tenure a remedy would be held up to the states, which altho' very distant, would probably keep them quiet. In aid of this a more immediate effect would be produced by a joint protestation of both Houses of Congress, that the doctrines of the judges in the case of Cohens, adjudging a state amenable to their tribunal, and that Congress can authorize a corporation of the district of Columbia to pass any act which shall have the force of law within a state, are contrary to the provisions of the Constitution of the U. S. This would be effectual; as with such an avowal of Congress, no state would permit such a sentence to be carried into execution, within its limits. If, by the distribution of the sovereign powers among three branches, they were intended to be checks on one another, the present case calls loudly for the exercise of that duty, and such a counter declaration, while proper in form, would be most salutary as a precedent.[6]

To William Johnson. Monticello, October 27, 1822.

Dear Sir—I have deferred my thanks for the copy of your Life of Genl. Greene, until I could have time to read it. This I have done, and with the greatest satisfaction; and can now more understandingly express the gratification it has afforded me. I really rejoice that we have at length a fair history of the Southern war. It proves how much we were left to defend ourselves as we could, while the resources of the Union were so disproportionately devoted to the North. I am glad too to see the Romance of Lee removed from the shelf of History to that of Fable. Some small portion of the transactions he relates were within my own knowledge; and of these I can say he has given more falsehood than fact; and I have heard many officers declare the same as to what had passed under their eyes. Yet this book had begun to be quoted as history. Greene was truly a great man, he had not perhaps all the qualities which so peculiarly rendered Genl. Washington the fittest man on earth for directing so great a contest under so great difficulties. Difficulties proceeding not from luke-warmness in our citizens or their functionaries, as our military leaders supposed; but from the pennyless condition of a people, totally shut out from all commerce and intercourse with the world, and therefore without any means for converting their labor into money. But Greene was second to no one in enterprise, in resource, in sound judgment, promptitude of decision, and every other military talent. In addition to the work you have given us, I look forward with anxiety to that you promise in the last paragraph of your book. Lee's military fable you have put down. Let not the invidious libel on the views of the Republican party, and on their regeneration of the government go down to posterity as hypocritically masked. I was myself too laboriously employed, while in office, and too old when I left it, to do justice to those who had labored so faithfully to arrest our course towards monarchy, and to secure the result of our revolutionary sufferings and sacrifices in a government bottomed on the only safe basis, the elective will of the people. You are young enough for the task, and I hope you will undertake it.

There is a subject respecting the practice of the court of which you are a member, which has long weighed on my mind, on which I have long thought I would write to you, and which I will take this opportunity of doing. It is in truth a delicate undertaking and yet such is my opinion of your candor and devotedness to the Constitution, in its true spirit, that I am sure I shall meet your approbation in unbosoming myself to you. The subject of my uneasiness is the habitual mode of making up and delivering the opinions of the supreme court of the U. S.

You know that from the earliest ages of the English law, from the date of the yearbooks, at least, to the end of the IId George, the judges of England, in all but self-evident cases, delivered their opinions seriatim, with the reasons and authorities which governed their decisions. If they sometimes consulted together, and gave a general opinion, it was so rarely as not to excite either alarm or notice. Besides the light which their separate arguments threw on the subject, and the instruction communicated by their several modes of reasoning, it shewed whether the judges were unanimous or divided, and gave accordingly more or less weight to the judgment as a precedent. It sometimes happened too that when there were three opinions against one, the reasoning of the one was so much the most cogent as to become afterwards the law of the land. When Ld. Mansfield came to the bench he introduced the habit of caucusing opinions. The judges met at their chambers, or elsewhere, secluded from the presence of the public, and made up what was to be delivered as the opinion of the court.

On the retirement of Mansfield, Ld. Kenyon put an end to the practice, and the judges returned to that of seriatim opinions, and practiced it habitually to this day, I believe. I am not acquainted with the late reporters, do not possess them, and state the fact from the information of others. To come now to ourselves I know nothing of what is done in other states, but in this our great and good Mr. Pendleton was, after the revolution, placed at the head of the court of Appeals. He adored Ld. Mansfield, and considered him as the greatest luminary of the law that any age had ever produced, and he introduced into the court over which he presided, Mansfield's practice of making up opinions in secret and delivering them as the Oracles of the court, in mass. Judge Roane, when he came to that bench, broke up the practice, refused to hatch judgments, in Conclave, or to let others deliver his opinions for him. At what time the seriatim opinions ceased in the supreme Court of the U. S., I am not informed. They continued I know to the end of the 3d Dallas in 1800. Later than which I have no Reporter of that court. About that time the present C. J. came to the bench. Whether he carried the practice of Mr. Pendleton to it, or who, or when I do not know; but I understand from others it is now the habit of the court, and I suppose it true from the cases sometimes reported in the newspapers, and others which I casually see, wherein I observe that the opinions were uniformly prepared in private. Some of the cases too have been of such importance, of such difficulty, and the decisions so grating to a portion of the public as to have merited the fullest explanation from every judge seriatim, of the reasons which had produced such convictions on his mind. It was interesting to the public to know whether these decisions were really unanimous, or might not perhaps be of 4 against 3 and consequently prevailing by the preponderance of one voice only. The Judges holding their offices for life are under two responsibilities only. 1. Impeachment. 2. Individual reputation. But this practice completely withdraws them from both. For nobody knows what opinion any individual member gave in any case, nor even that he who delivers the opinion, concurred in it himself. Be the opinion therefore ever so impeachable, having been done in the dark it can be proved on no one. As to the 2d guarantee, personal reputation, it is shielded completely. The practice is certainly convenient for the lazy, the modest and the incompetent. It saves them the trouble of developing their opinion methodically and even of making up an opinion at all. That of seriatim argument shows whether every judge has taken the trouble of understanding the case, of investigating it minutely, and of forming an opinion for himself, instead of pinning it on another's sleeve. It would certainly be right to abandon this practice in order to give to our citizens one and all, that confidence in their judges which must be so desirable to the judges themselves, and so important to the cement of the union. During the administration of Genl. Washington, and while E. Randolph was Attorney General, he was required by Congress to digest the judiciary laws into a single one, with such amendments as might be thought proper. He prepared a section requiring the Judges to give their opinions seriatim, in writing, to be recorded in a distinct volume. Other business prevented this bill from being taken up, and it passed off, but such a volume would have been the best possible book of reports, and the better, as unincumbered with the hired sophisms and perversions of Counsel.[7]

To William Johnson. Monticello, June 12, 1823.

You request me confidentially, to examine the question, whether the Supreme Court has advanced beyond its constitutional limits, and trespassed on those of the State authorities? I do not undertake it, my dear Sir, because I am unable. Age and the wane of mind consequent on it, have disqualified me from investigations so severe, and researches so laborious. And it is the less necessary in this case, as having been already done by others with a logic and learning to which I could add nothing. On the decision of the case of Cohens *vs.* The State of Virginia, in the Supreme Court of the United States, in March, 1821, Judge Roane, under the signature of Algeron Sidney, wrote for the *Enquirer* a series of papers on the law of that case. I considered these papers maturely as they came out, and confess that they appeared to me to pulverize every word which had been delivered by Judge Marshall, of the extra-judicial part of his opinion; and all was extra-judicial, except the decision that the act of Congress had not purported to give to the corporation of Washington the authority claimed by their lottery law, of controlling the laws of the States within the States themselves. But unable to claim that case, he could not let it go entirely, but went on gratuitously to prove, that notwithstanding the eleventh amendment of the constitution, a State *could* be brought as a defendant, to the bar of his court; and again, that Congress might authorize a corporation of its territory to exercise legislation within a State, and paramount to the laws of that State. I cite the sum and result only of his doctrines, according to the impression made on my mind at the time, and still remaining. If not strictly accurate in circumstance, it is so in substance. This doctrine was so completely refuted by Roane, that if he can be answered, I surrender human reason as a vain and useless faculty, given to bewilder, and not to guide us. And I mention this particular case as one only of several, because it gave occasion to that thorough examination of the constitutional limits between the General and State jurisdictions, which you have asked for. There were two other writers in the same paper, under the signatures of Fletcher of Saltoun, and Somers, who, in a few essays, presented some very luminous and striking views of the question. And there was a particular paper which recapitulated all the cases in which it was thought the federal court had usurped on the State jurisdictions. These essays will be found in the *Enquirers* of 1821, from May the 10th to July the 13th. It is not in my present power to send them to you, but if Ritchie can furnish them, I will procure and forward them. If they had been read in the other States, as they were here, I think they would have left, there as here, no dissentients from their doctrine. The subject was taken up by our legislature of 1821-'22, and two draughts of remonstrances were prepared and discussed. As well as I remember, there was no difference of opinion as to the matter of right; but there was as to the expediency of a remonstrance at that time, the general mind of the States being then under extraordinary excitement by the Missouri question; and it was dropped on that consideration. But this case is not dead, it only sleepeth. The Indian Chief said he did not go to war for every petty injury by itself, but put it into his pouch, and when that was full, he made war. Thank Heaven, we have provided a more peaceable and rational mode of redress.

This practice of Judge Marshall, of travelling out of his case to prescribe what the law would be in a moot case not before the court, is very irregular and very censurable. I recollect another instance, and the more particularly, perhaps, because it in some measure bore on myself. Among the midnight appointments of Mr. Adams, were commissions to some federal justices of the peace for Alexandria. These were signed and sealed by him, but not delivered. I found them on the table of the department of State, on my entrance into office, and I forbade their delivery. Marbury, named in one of them applied to the Supreme Court for a mandamus to the Secretary of State, (Mr. Madison) to deliver the commission intended for him. The court determined at once, that being an original process, they had no cognizance of it; and therefore the question before them was ended. But the Chief Justice went on to lay down what the law would be, had they jurisdiction of the case, to wit: that they should command the delivery. The object was clearly to instruct any other court having the jurisdiction, what they should do if Marbury should apply to them. Besides the impropriety of this gratuitous interference, could anything exceed the perversion of law? For if there is any principle of law never yet contradicted, it is that delivery is one of the essentials to the validity of the deed. Although signed and sealed, yet as long as it remains in the hands of the party himself, it is in *fieri* only, it is not a deed, and can be made so only by its delivery. In the hands of a third person it may be made an escrow. But whatever is in the executive offices is certainly deemed to be in the hands of the President; and in this case, was actually in my hands, because, when I countermanded them, there was as yet no Secretary of State. Yet this case of Marbury and Madison is continually cited by bench and bar, as if it were settled law, without any animadversion on its being merely an *obiter* dissertation of the Chief Justice.

It may be impracticable to lay down any general formula of words which shall decide at once, and with precision, in every case, this limit of jurisdiction. But there are two canons which will guide us safely in most cases. 1st., The capital and leading object of the constitution was to leave with the States all authorities which respected their own citizens only, and to transfer to the United States those which respected citizens of foreign or other States: to make us several as to ourselves, but one as to all others. In the latter case, then, constructions should lean to the general jurisdiction, if the words will bear it; and in favor of the States in the former, if possible to be so construed. And indeed, between citizens and citizens of the same State, and under their own laws, I know but a single case in which a jurisdiction is given to the General Government. That is, where anything but gold or silver is made lawful tender, or the obligation of contracts is any otherwise impaired. The separate legislatures had so often abused that power, that the citizens themselves chose to trust it to the general, rather than to their own special authorities. 2d., On every question of construction, carry ourselves back to the time when the constitution was adopted, recollect the spirit manifested in the debates, and instead of trying what meaning may be squeezed out of the text, or invented against it, conform to the probable one in which it was passed. Let us try Cohen's case by these canons only, referring always, however, for full argument, to the essays before cited.

1. It was between a citizen and his own State, and under a law of his State. It was a domestic case, therefore, and not a foreign one.

2. Can it be believed, that under the jealousies prevailing against the General Government, at the adoption of the constitution, the States meant to surrender the authority of preserving order, of enforcing moral duties and restraining vice, within their own territory? And this is the present case, that of Cohen being under the ancient and general law of gaming. Can any good be effected by taking from the States the moral rule of their citizens, and subordinating it to the general authority, or to one of their corporations, which may justify forcing the meaning of words, hunting after possible constructions, and hanging inference on inference, from heaven to earth, like Jacob's ladder? Such an intention was impossible, and such a licentiousness of construction and inference, if exercised by both governments, as may be done with equal right, would equally authorize both to claim all power, general and particular, and break up the foundations of the Union. Laws are made for men of ordinary understanding, and should, therefore, be construed by the ordinary rules of

common sense. Their meaning is not to be sought for in metaphysical subtleties, which may make anything mean everything or nothing, at pleasure. It should be left to the sophisms of advocates, whose trade it is, to prove that a defendant is a plaintiff, though dragged into court, *torto collo,* like Bonaparte's volunteers, into the field in chains, or that a power has been given, because it ought to have been given, *et alia talia.* The States supposed that by their tenth amendment, they had secured themselves against constructive powers. They were not lessened yet by Cohen's case, nor aware of the slipperiness of the eels of the law. I ask for no straining of words against the General Government, nor yet against the States. I believe the States can best govern our home concerns, and the General Government our foreign ones. I wish, therefore, to see maintained that wholesome distribution of powers established by the constitution for the limitation of both; and never to see all offices transferred to Washington, where, further withdrawn from the eyes of the people, they may more secretly be bought and sold as at market.

But the Chief Justice says, "there must be an ultimate arbiter somewhere." True, there must; but does that prove it is either party? The ultimate arbiter is the people of the Union, assembled by their deputies in convention, at the call of Congress, or of two-thirds of the States. Let them decide to which they mean to give an authority claimed by two of their organs. And it has been the peculiar wisdom and felicity of our constitution, to have provided this peaceable appeal, where that of other nations is at once to force.

I rejoice in the example you set of *seriatim* opinions. I

have heard it often noticed, and always with high approbation. Some of your brethren will be encouraged to follow it occasionally, and in time, it may be felt by all as a duty, and the sound practice of the primitive court be again restored. Why should not every judge be asked his opinion, and give it from the bench, if only by yea or nay? Besides ascertaining the fact of his opinion, which the public have a right to know, in order to judge whether it is impeachable or not, it would show whether the opinions were unanimous or not, and thus settle more exactly the weight of their authority.[8]

Jefferson's views on slavery were well known throughout his political career. He described the institution of slavery in this country in his Notes on Virginia *as "the most unremitting despotism" and introduced a bill in the Virginia Legislature for the emancipation of the slaves. Jefferson anticipated that the United States would finally come to be divided geographically on this question. In 1820 an amendment was adopted on the motion of J. B. Thomas of Illinois to exclude slavery from the Louisiana Purchase north of 36⁰ 30″ except within the limits of the proposed state of Missouri. The House of Representatives refused to accept this amendment but an act of admission—sometimes referred to as the second Missouri Compromise—was finally passed through the influence of Henry Clay.*

Slavery and the Missouri Question

Notes on Virginia.

There must doubtless be an unhappy influence on the manners of our people produced by the existence of slavery among us. The whole commerce between master and slave is a perpetual exercise of the most boisterous passions, the most unremitting despotism on the one part, and degrading submissions on the other. Our children see this, and learn to imitate it; for man is an imitative animal. This quality is the germ of all education in him . . . The man must be a prodigy who can retain his manners and morals undepraved by such circumstances. And with what execrations should the statesman be loaded, who permitting one half the citizens thus to trample on the rights of the other, transforms those into despots, and these into enemies, destroys the morals of the one part, and the *amor patriae* of the other. For if a slave can have a country in this world, it must be any other in preference to that in which he is born to live and labor for another: in which he must lock up the faculties of his nature, contribute as far as depends on his individual endeavors to the evanishment of the human race, or entail his own miserable condition on the endless generations proceeding from him. With the morals of the people, their industry also is de-

235

stroyed. For in a warm climate, no man will labor for himself who can make another labor for him. This is so true, that of the proprietors of slaves a very small proportion indeed are ever seen to labor. And can the liberties of a nation be thought secure when we have removed their only firm basis, a conviction in the minds of the people that these liberties are of the gift of God? That they are not to be violated but with his wrath? Indeed I tremble for my country when I reflect that God is just: that his justice cannot sleep forever: that considering numbers, nature and natural means only, a revolution of the wheel of fortune, an exchange of situation, is among possible events: that it may become probable by supernatural interference! The Almighty has no attribute which can take side with us in such a contest.—But it is impossible to be temperate and to pursue this subject through the various considerations of policy, of morals, of history natural and civil. We must be contented to hope they will force their way into every one's mind. I think a change already perceptible, since the origin of the present revolution. The spirit of the master is abating, that of the slave rising from the dust, his condition mollifying, the way I hope preparing, under the auspices of heaven, for a total emancipation, and that this is disposed, in the order of events, to be with the consent of the masters, rather than by their extirpation.[1]

To George Washington. Philadelphia, May 23, 1792.

I can scarcely contemplate a more incalculable evil than the breaking of the union into two or more parts. Yet when we review the mass which opposed the original coalescence, when we consider that it lay chiefly in the Southern quarter, that the legislature have availed themselves of no occasion of allaying it, but on the contrary whenever Northern and Southern prejudices have come into conflict, the latter have been sacrificed and the former soothed; that the owners of the debt are in the Southern and the holders of it in the Northern division; that the Anti-federal champions are now strengthened in argument by the fulfilment of their predictions; that this has been brought about by the Monarchical federalists themselves, who, having been for the new government merely as a stepping stone to monarchy, have themselves adopted the very constitution, of which, when advocating its acceptance before the tribunal of the people, they declared it insusceptible; that the republican federalists, who espoused the same government for its intrinsic merits, are disarmed of their weapons, that which they denied as prophecy being now become true history: who can be sure that these things may not proselyte the small number which was wanting to place the majority on the other side? And this is the event at which I tremble, and to prevent which I consider your continuance at the head of affairs as of the last importance. The confidence of the whole union is centered in you. Your being at the helm, will be more than an answer to every argument which can be used to alarm and lead the people in any quarter into violence or secession. North and South will hang together, if they have you to hang on . . .[2]

To St. George Tucker. Monticello, August 28, 1797.

Dear Sir—I have to acknowledge the receipt of your two favors of the 2d and 22d inst. and to thank you for the pamphlet covered by the former. You know my sub-scription to its doctrines; and to the mode of emancipation, I am satisfied that that must be a matter of compromise between the passions, the prejudices, and the real diffi-culties which will each have their weight in that operation. Perhaps the first chapter of this history, which has begun in St. Domingo, and the next succeeding ones, which will recount how all the whites were driven from all the other islands, may prepare our minds for a peaceable accommo-dation between justice, policy and necessity; and furnish an answer to the difficult question whither shall the colored emigrants go? and the sooner we put some plan underway, the greater hope there is that it may be permitted to pro-ceed peaceably to its ultimate effect. But if something is not done, and soon done, we shall be the murderers of our own children. The *"murmura venturos nautis prodentia ventos"* has already reached us; the revolutionary storm, now sweeping the globe, will be upon us, and happy if we make timely provision to give it an easy passage over our land. From the present state of things in Europe and America, the day which begins our combustion must be near at hand; and only a single spark is wanting to make that day tomorrow. If we had begun sooner, we might probably have been allowed a lengthier operation to clear ourselves, but every day's delay lessens the time we may take for emancipation. Some people derive hope from the aid of the confederated States. But this is a delusion. There is but one state in the Union which will aid us sincerely, if an insurrection begins, and that one may, perhaps, have its own fire to quench at the same time.[3]

To William A. Burwell, Washington, January 28, 1805.

Dear Sir—Your letter of the 18th has been duly received and Mr. Coles consents to remain here till the 4th of March, when I shall leave this place for Monticello and pass a month there. Consequently if you can join me here the second week in April it will be as early as your absence could affect my convenience. I have long since given up the expectation of any early provision for the extinguishment of slavery among us. There are many virtuous men who would make any sacrifices to effect it, many equally virtuous who persuade themselves either that the thing is not wrong, or that it cannot be remedied, and very many with whom interest is morality. The older we grow, the larger we are disposed to believe the last party to be. But interest is really going over to the side of morality. The value of the slave is every day lessening; his burden on his master daily increasing. Interest is therefore preparing the disposition to be just; and this will be goaded from time to time by the insurrectionary spirit of the slaves. This is easily quelled in its first efforts; but from being local it will become general, and whenever it does it will rise more formidable after every defeat, until we shall be forced, after dreadful scenes and sufferings to release them in their own way, which, without such sufferings we might now model after our own convenience.[4]

To Dr. Thomas Humphreys. Monticello, February 8, 1817.

Dear Sir—Your favor of January 2d did not come to my hands until the 5th instant. I concur entirely in your leading principles of gradual emancipation, of establishment on the coast of Africa, and the patronage of our nation until the emigrants shall be able to protect themselves. The subordinate details might be easily arranged. But the bare proposition of purchase by the United States generally, would excite infinite indignation in all the States north of Maryland. The sacrifice must fall on the States alone which hold them; and the difficult question will be how to lessen this so as to reconcile our fellow citizens to it. Personally I am ready and desirous to make any sacrifice which shall ensure their gradual but complete retirement from the State, and effectually, at the same time, establish them elsewhere in freedom and safety. But I have not perceived the growth of this disposition in the rising generation, of which I once had sanguine hopes. No symptoms inform me that it will take place in my day. I leave it, therefore, to time, and not at all without hope that the day will come, equally desirable and welcome to us as to them. Perhaps the proposition now on the carpet at Washington to provide an establishment on the coast of Africa for voluntary emigrations of people of color, may be the corner stone of this future edifice. Praying for its completion as early as may most promote the good of all, I salute you with great esteem and respect.[5]

To Hugh Nelson. Monticello, March 12, 1820.

I thank you, dear Sir, for the information in your favor of the 4th instant, of the settlement, *for the present,* of the Missouri question. I am so completely withdrawn from all attention to public matters, that nothing less could arouse me than the definition of a geographical line, which on an abstract principle is to become the line of separation of these States, and to render desperate the hope that man can ever enjoy the two blessings of peace and self-government. The question sleeps for the present, but is not dead.[6]

To Albert Gallatin. Monticello, December 26, 1820.

The steady tenor of the courts of the United States to break down the constitutional barriers between the coordinate powers of the States and of the Union, and a formal opinion lately given by five lawyers of too much eminence to be neglected, give uneasiness. But nothing has ever presented so threatening an aspect as what is called the Missouri question. The Federalists, completely put down and despairing of ever rising again under the old divisions of Whig and Tory, devised a new one of slave-holding and non-slave holding States, which, while it had the semblance of being moral, was at the same time geographical, and calculated to give them ascendency by debauching their old opponents to a coalition with them. Moral the question certainly is not, because the removal of slaves from one State to another, no more than their removal from one country to another, would never make a slave of one human being who would not be so without it. Indeed, if there were any morality in the question it is on the other side; because by spreading them over a larger surface their happiness would be increased, and burden of their future liberation lightened by bringing a greater number of shoulders under it. However, it served to throw dust into the eyes of the people and to fanaticize them, while to the knowing ones it gave a geographical and preponderant line of the Potomac and Ohio, throwing fourteen States to the North and East, and ten to the South and West. With these, therefore, it is merely a question of power; but with geographical minority it is a question of existence. For if Congress once goes out of the Constitution to arrogate a right of regulating the condition of the inhabitants of the States, its majority may, and probably will, next declare that the condition of all men within the United States shall be that of freedom; in which case all the whites south of the Potomac and Ohio must evacuate their States and most fortunate those who can do it first. And so far this crisis seems to be advancing. The Missouri constitution is recently rejected by the House of Representatives; what will be their next step is yet to be seen. If accepted on the condition that Missouri shall expunge from it the prohibition of free people of color from emigration to their State, it will be expunged, and all will be quieted until the advance of some new State, shall present the question again. If rejected unconditionally, Missouri assumes independent self-government, and Congress, after pouting awhile, must receive them on the footing of the original States. Should the Representatives propose force, 1, the Senate will not concur; 2, were they to concur, there would be a secession of the members south of the line, and probably of the three Northwestern States, who, however inclined to the other side, would scarcely separate from those who would hold the Mississippi from its mouth to its source. What next? Conjecture itself is at a loss. But whatever it shall be you will hear from others and from the newspapers; and finally the whole will depend on Pennsylvania. While she and Virginia hold together, the Atlantic States can never separate. Unfortunately, in the present case she has become more fanaticized than any other State. However useful where you are, I wish you were with them. You might turn the scale there, which would turn it for the whole. Should this scission take place, one of the most deplorable consequences would be its discouragement of the efforts of the European nations in the regeneration of their oppressive and cannibal governments. Amidst this prospect of evil I am glad to see one good effect. It has brought the necessity of some plan of general emancipation and deportation more home to the minds of our people than it has ever been before, insomuch that our governor has ventured to propose one to the Legislature. This will probably not be acted on at this time, nor would it be effectual; for, while it proposes to devote to that object one-third of the revenue of the State, it would not reach one-tenth of the annual increase. My proposition would be that the holders should give up all born after a certain day, past, present, or to come; that these should be placed under the guardianship of the State, and sent at a proper age to St. Domingo. They are willing to receive them, and the shortness of the passage brings the deportation within the possible means of taxation, aided by charitable contributions. In these I think Europe, which has forced this evil on us, and the Eastern States, who have been its chief instruments of importation, would be bound to give largely. But the proceeds of the land office, if appropriate to this, would be quite sufficient.[7]

In letters to James Monroe, Alexander Von Humbolt and Joseph Priestley, Jefferson comes to several conclusions. He anticipates our war with Spain eighty years before the event and previews the possible geographic division of inpendent states in South America. In his letter to Joseph Priestley, Jefferson mentions the unique event—something new under the sun—of a sovereign government of the people proving itself under great stress and sustaining his conviction that it was, in fact, the strongest government on earth.

Conclusions

To James Monroe. Monticello, February 4, 1816.

Dear Sir—Your letter concerning that of General Scott is received, and his is now returned. I am very thankful for these communications. From forty years' experience of the wretched guess-work of the newspapers of what is not done in open day-light, and of their falsehood even as to that, I rarely think them worth reading, and almost never worth notice. A ray, therefore, now and then, from the fountain of light, is like sight restored to the blind. It tells me where I am; and that to a mariner who has long been without sight of land or sun, is a rallying of reckoning which places him at ease. The ground you have taken from Spain is sound in every part. It is the true ground, especially, as to the South Americans. When subjects are able to maintain themselves in the field, they are then an independent power as to all neutral nations, are entitled to their commerce, and to protection within their limits. Every kindness which can be shown the South Americans, every friendly office and aid within the limits of the law of nations, I would extend to them, without fearing Spain or her Swiss auxiliaries. For this is but an assertion of our own independence. But to join in their war, as General Scott proposes, and to which even some members of Congress seem to squint, is what we ought not to do as yet. On the question of our interests in their independence, were that alone a sufficient motive of action, much may be said on both sides. When they are free, they will drive every article of our produce from every market, by underselling it, and change the condition of our existence, forcing us into other habits and pursuits. We shall, indeed, have in exchange some commerce with them, but in what I know not, for we shall have nothing to offer which they cannot raise cheaper; and their separation from Spain seals our everlasting peace with her. On the other hand, so long as they are dependent, Spain, from her jealousy, is our natural enemy, and always in either open or secret hostility with us. These countries, too, in war, will be a powerful weight in her scale, and, in peace, totally shut to us. Interest then, on the whole, would wish their independence, and justice makes the wish a duty. They have a right to be free, and we a right to aid them, as a strong man has a right to assist a weak one assailed by a robber or murderer. That a war is brewing between us and Spain cannot be doubted. When that disposition is matured on both sides, and open rupture can no longer be deferred, then will be the time for our joining the South Americans, and entering into treaties of alliance with them. There will then be but one opinion, at home or abroad, that we shall be justifiable in choosing to have them with us, rather than against us. In the meantime they will have organized regular governments, and perhaps have formed themselves into one or more confederacies; more than one I hope, as in a single mass they would be a very formidable neighbor. The geography of their country seems to indicate three: 1. What is north of the Isthmus. 2. What is south of it on the Atlantic; and and 3. The southern part on the Pacific. In this form, we might be the balancing power.[1]

To Baron F. H. Alexander Von Humboldt.

Monticello, June 13, 1817.

Dear Sir—The receipt of your *Distributio Geographica Plantarum,* with the duty of thanking you for a work which sheds so much new and valuable light on botanical science, excites the desire, also, of presenting myself to your recollection, and of expressing to you those sentiments of high admiration and esteem, which, although long silent, have never slept. The physical information you have given us of a country hitherto so shamefully unknown, has come exactly in time to guide our understandings in the great political revolution now bringing it into prominence on the stage of the world. The issue of its struggles, as they respect Spain, is no longer matter of doubt. As it respects their own liberty, peace and happiness, we cannot be quite so certain. Whether the blinds of bigotry, the shackles of the priesthood, and the fascinating glare of rank and wealth, give fair play to the common sense of the mass of their people, so far as to qualify them for self-government, is what we do not know. Perhaps our wishes may be stronger than our hopes. The first principle of republicanism is, that the *lex-majoris partis* is the fundamental law of every society of individuals of equal rights; to consider the will of the society announced by the majority of a single vote, as sacred as if unanimous, is the first of all lessons in importance, yet the last which is thoroughly learnt. This law once disregarded, no other remains but that of force, which ends necessarily in military despotism. This has been the history of the French revolution, and I wish the understanding of our Southern brethren may be sufficiently enlarged and firm to see that their fate depends on its sacred observance.

In our America we are turning to public improvements. Schools, roads, and canals, are everywhere either in operation or contemplation. The most gigantic undertaking yet proposed, is that of New York, for drawing the waters of Lake Erie into the Hudson. The distance is 353 miles, and the height to be surmounted 661 feet. The expense will be great, but its effect incalculably powerful in favor of the Atlantic States. Internal navigation by steamboats is rapidly spreading through all our States, and that by sails and oars will ere long be looked back to as among the curiosities of antiquity. We count much, too, on its efficacy for harbour defense; and it will soon be tried for navigation by sea. We consider the employment of the contributions which our citizens can spare, after feeding, and clothing, and lodging themselves comfortably, as more useful, more moral, and even more splendid, than that preferred by Europe, of destroying human life, labor and happiness.[2]

To Joseph Priestley. Washington. March 21, 1801.

As the storm is now subsiding, and the horizon becoming serene, it is pleasant to consider the phenomenon with attention. We can no longer say there is nothing new under the sun. For this whole chapter in the history of man is new. The great extent of our Republic is new. Its sparse habitation is new. The mighty wave of public opinion which has rolled over it is new. But the most pleasing novelty is, it's so quickly subsiding over such an extent of surface to its true level again. The order and good sense displayed in this recovery from delusion, and in the momentous crisis which lately arose, really bespeak a strength of character in our nation which augers well for the duration of our Republic; and I am much better satisfied now of its stability than I was before it was tried.[3]

Bibliography

Bowers, Claude G. *Jefferson in Power*. Boston, 1936.

Boyd, Julian P., editor. *The Papers of Thomas Jefferson*. Princeton University Press, Princeton, 1950.

Cappon, Lester J., editor. *The Adams-Jefferson Letters*. 2 vols. University of North Carolina Press, Chapel Hill, 1959.

Chinard, Gilbert. *Thomas Jefferson The Apostle of Americanism*. Boston, 1929.

Dos Passos, John. *The Head and Heart of Thomas Jefferson*. New York, 1954.

Fleming, Thomas. *The Man from Monticello*. New York, 1969.

Ford, Paul Leicester, editor. *The Writings of Thomas Jefferson*. 10 vols. New York, 1889.

Forman, S. E. *The Life and Writings of Thomas Jefferson*. Indianapolis, 1900.

Malone, Dumas. *Jefferson the Virginian*. Boston, 1948.

——*Jefferson and the Rights of Man*. Boston, 1951.

Nock, Albert J. *Jefferson*. New York, 1926.

Peterson, Merrill D. *The Jefferson Image in the American Mind*. New York, 1960.

——*Thomas Jefferson and the New Nation*. New York, 1970.

Randall, Henry S. *The Life of Thomas Jefferson*. 3 vols. New York, 1858.

Randolph, T. J., editor. *Memoirs, Correspondence and Miscellanies from the Papers of Thomas Jefferson.* 4 vols. Boston, 1830.

Washington, H. A., editor. *The Works of Thomas Jefferson.* 9 vols. Congressional Edition. New York, 1884.

Wiltse, Charles Maurice. *The Jeffersonian Tradition in American Democracy.* New York, 1960.

Works. *The Writings of Thomas Jefferson.* 20 vols. Washington, 1903.

References

INTRODUCTION

1. Ford, Paul Leicester, editor. *The Writings of Thomas Jefferson.* 1889. 10 vols. X., p. 281.

2. Randall, Henry S. *The Life of Thomas Jefferson.* 1858. 3 vols. II., p. 267.

3. Peterson, Merrill D. *The Jefferson Image.* New York, 1960. p. 335.

4. Peterson, Merrill D. *Thomas Jefferson and the New Nation.* 1970. p. 316.

5. Peterson, Merrill D. *The Jefferson Image.* New York, 1960. p. 335.

6. *Ibid.,* p. 162

7. *Congressional Edition of Jefferson's Works.* New York, 1884. 9 vols. VI., p. 591.

8. Nikhilananda, Swami. *Self-Knowledge* (Atmabodha). New York, 1946. p. xiii.

9. *Congressional Edition.* 1884. V., p. 396.

10. Ford. *Writings.* I., p. 134.

11. *Ibid.,* V., p. 2.

12. *Ibid.,* X., p. 332.

13. *Ibid.,* VII., p. 32.

14. *Ibid.,* VI., p. 102.

15. *Ibid.,* VII., p. 15.

16. *Ibid.,* VII., p. 75.

17. Chinard, Gilbert. *Thomas Jefferson The Apostle of Americanism.* Boston, 1929. p. 339.

18. Ford. *Writings.* VII., p. 309.

19. *Ibid.,* VII., p. 355.
20. *Ibid.,* VII., p. 337.
21. Forman, S. E. *The Life and Writings of Thomas Jefferson.* (1900). p. 83.
22. Ford. *Writings.* VII., p. 491.
23. Forman. *Life.* p. 245.
24. *Ibid.,* p. 85.
25. Peterson. *Thomas Jefferson.* p. 659.
26. Ford. *Writings.* VII., p. 145.
27. Peterson. *Thomas Jefferson.* p. 760.

THE RIGHTS OF MAN

1. Ford. *Writings.* X., p. 342.
2. *Congressional Edition.* 1884. VI., p. 143.
3. *Writings of Thomas Jefferson.* Washington, 1903. 20 vols. XV., p. 482.
4. *Ibid.,* XI., p. 52.
5. Ford. *Writings.* V., p. 76.
6. *Ibid.,* VIII., p. 150.
7. *Writings.* 1903. VI., p. 425.
8. Ford. *Writings.* V., p. 253.
9. *Ibid.,* IV., p. 473.
10. *Ibid.,* III., p. 254.

MINISTER TO FRANCE

1. *Writings.* 1903. V., p. 396.
2. Ford. *Writings.* IV., p. 59.
3. *Ibid.,* IV., p. 68.
4. *Ibid.,* V., p. 293.
5. Randolph, T. J., editor. *Memoirs, Correspondence*

and Miscellanies. Boston, 1830. 4 vols. I., p. 396.

6. *Writings.* 1903. V., p. 395.
7. Ford. *Writings.* IV., p. 466.
8. *Ibid.,* IV., p. 87.
9. *Ibid.,* V., p. 2.
10. *Ibid.,* V., p. 107.
11. *Ibid.,* V., p. 45.
12. *Ibid.,* IV., p. 426.
13. *Writings.* 1903. VII., p. 422.
14. Randolph. *Memoirs.* II., p. 493.
15. Ford. *Writings.* V., p. 74.
16. *Ibid.,* V., p. 88.
17. *Ibid.,* V., p. 377.
18. *Ibid.,* VI., p. 96.
19. *Ibid.,* V., p. 153.
20. *Congressional Edition.* 1884. VII., p. 235.
21. Ford. *Writings.* IV., p. 67.
22. Randolph. *Memoirs.* IV., p. 160.

PARTY DIVISIONS

1. Ford. *Writings.* X., p. 332.
2. Forman. *Life and Writings.* p. 365.
3. *Ibid.,* p. 366.
4. *Ibid.,* p. 366.
5. Ford. *Writings.* V., p. 94.
6. *Ibid.,* V., p. 300.
7. *Congressional Edition.* 1884. VI., p. 97.
8. *Writings.* 1903. XIV., p. 142.
9. Ford. *Writings.* VII., p. 35.
10. *Ibid.,* II., p. 131.

11. *Ibid.,* V., p. 83.
12. *Ibid.,* VI., p. 87.
13. *Ibid.,* VII., p. 304.
14. *Ibid.,* III., p. 265.
15. *Congressional Edition.* 1884. VII., p. 198.
16. Ford. *Writings.* VII., p. 203.
17. *Ibid.,* VII., p. 453.
18. *Ibid.,* II., p. 14.
19. *Congressional Edition.* 1884. VI., p. 592.
20. Ford. *Writings.* VIII., p. 355.
21. *Ibid.,* VIII., p. 158.
22. *Congressional Edition.* 1884. VI., p. 464
23. Ford. *Writings.* VII., p. 416.
24. Forman. *Life and Writings.* p. 302.
25. *Ibid.,* p. 301.
26. Ford. *Writings.* VII., p. 451.
27. *Ibid.,* IX., p. 71.
28. *Ibid.,* V., p. 173.
29. *Congressional Edition.* 1884. VI., p. 45.
30. *Ibid.,* VI., p. 591.
32. Ford. *Writings.* VII., p. 2.
33. *Writings.* 1903. XIV., p. 396.
34. Ford. *Writings.* X., p. 372.
35. *Congressional Edition.* 1884. V., p. 390.

ALIEN & SEDITION LAWS

1. Ford. *Writings.* VI., 244.
2. Randolph. *Memoirs.* III., p. 388.
3. *Ibid.* III., p. 390.
4. Ford. *Writings.* VII., p. 266.

5. Randolph. *Memoirs.* III., p. 401.
6. Ford. *Writings.* VII., p. 283.
7. *Ibid.,* VII., p. 289.
8. *Writings.* 1903. XIV., p. 127.
9. Ford. *Writings.* IX., p. 456.
10. *Ibid.,* VII., p. 290.

LETTERS FROM THE PRESIDENT

1. Randolph. *Memoirs.* III., p. 452.
2. *Ibid.,* III., p. 454.
3. Ford. *Writings.* VIII., p. 26.
4. *Ibid.,* VIII., p. 139.
5. Ford. *Writings.* V., p. 53.
6. *Congressional Edition.* 1884. VIII., p. 145.
7. Ford. *Writings.* VII., p. 447.
8. *Ibid.,* IX., p. 71.
9. *Ibid.,* VIII., p. 292.
10. *Ibid.,* VIII., p. 305.

MISSISSIPPI & LOUISIANA TERRITORIES

1. Ford. *Writings.* IV., p. 179.
2. *Ibid.,* IV., p. 363.
3. Randolph. *Memoirs.* II., p. 316.
4. Ford. *Writings.* V., p. 225.
5. Randolph. *Memoirs.* III., p. 220.
6. Ford. *Writings.* VIII., p. 144.
7. *Ibid.,* VIII., p. 192.
8. *Ibid.,* VIII., p. 249.
9. *Ibid.,* I., p. 299.
10. *Ibid.,* VIII., p. 243.

11. *Ibid.,* VIII., p. 262.
12. *Ibid.,* VIII., p. 286.
13. *Ibid.,* VIII., p. 245.
14. *Ibid.,* VIII., p. 245.
15. *Ibid.,* VIII., p. 245.
16. *Ibid.,* VIII., p. 246.
17. *Ibid.,* VIII., p. 247.
18. *Ibid.,* VIII., p. 283.
19. *Ibid.,* VIII., p. 419.
20. *Ibid.,* IX., p. 8.
23. *Ibid.,* X., p. 154.
21. *Ibid.,* X., p. 20.
22. *Ibid.,* X., p. 114.

ON THE ECONOMY

1. Ford. *Writings.* IX., p. 488.
2. *Ibid.,* IX., p. 496.
3. *Ibid.,* X., p. 7.
4. *Ibid.,* X., p. 133.
5. *Ibid.,* X., p. 156.
6. *Ibid.,* X., p. 156.
7. *Ibid.,* X., p. 176.

GOVERNMENT & THE CONSTITUTION

1. Ford. *Writings.* X., p. 37.
2. *Ibid.* X., p. 45.
3. *Ibid.,* X., p. 225.
4. *Ibid.,* X., p. 226.

PARTY LEADERS & THE REVOLUTION

1. Ford. *Writings.* V., p. 7.
2. *Congressional Edition.* 1884. IX., p. 96.
3. Ford. *Writings.* III., p. 310.
4. *Ibid.,* V., p. 329.
5. *Ibid.,* VII., p. 425.
6. *Ibid.,* V., p. 353.
7. *Ibid.,* IX., p. 102.
8. *Ibid.,* IX., p. 455.
9. *Ibid.,* IX., p. 507.
10. *Ibid.,* IX., p. 526.
11. *Ibid.,* IX., p. 532.

FOREIGN WARS & TREATIES

1. Ford. *Writings.* V., p. 481.
2. Randolph. *Memoirs.* III., p. 391.
3. Ford. *Writings.* VII., p. 374.
4. *Ibid.,* VIII., p. 62.
5. *Ibid.,* VIII., p. 350.
6. *Ibid.,* VIII., p. 377.
7. *Ibid.,* IX., p. 271.
8. *Ibid.,* IX., p. 319.
9. *Congressional Edition.* 1884. VI., p. 453.
10. Ford. *Writings.* IX., p. 504.
11. *Ibid.* IX., p. 528.
12. *Ibid.,* X., p. 7.
13. *Ibid.,* X., p. 11.
14. *Ibid.,* X., p. 155.
15. *Ibid.,* X., p. 175.
16. Randolph. *Memoirs.* I., p. 292.

17. Ford. *Writings.* V., p. 22.
18. *Ibid.,* V., p. 198.

THE JUDICIARY

1. Ford. *Writings.* II., p. 59.
2. *Ibid.,* IV., p. 402.
3. *Ibid.,* X., p. 140.
4. *Ibid.,* X., p. 160.
5. *Ibid.,* X., p. 169.
6. *Ibid.,* X., p. 198.
7. *Ibid.,* X., p. 222.
8. *Ibid.,* X., p. 229.

SLAVERY & THE MISSOURI QUESTION

1. Ford. *Writings.* III., p. 266.
2. *Ibid.,* VI., p. 4.
3. *Ibid.,* VII., p. 167.
4. *Ibid.,* VIII., p. 340.
5. *Ibid.,* X., p. 76.
6. *Ibid.,* X., p. 156.
7. *Ibid.,* X., p. 175.

CONCLUSIONS

1. Ford. *Writings.* X., p. 18.
2. *Ibid.,* X., p. 88.
3. *Ibid.,* VIII., p. 22.